WORDPERFECT 5.1
Training Guide

Carol Elston & Sue Orrell

D1825456

PITMAN PUBLISHING

PITMAN PUBLISHING
128 Long Acre, London, WC2E 9AN
Pitman Publishing
A Division of Longman Group UK Limited

© Carol Elston & Sue Orrell 1992

First published in Great Britain 1992
Reprinted 1992
Reprinted 1993 (twice)

British Library Cataloguing in Publication Data
Elston, Carol
    Wordperfect 5.1. – (Training guide series)
    I. Title II. Orrell, Sue III. Series
    652.5

ISBN 0-273-03747-1

Printed in England by Clays Ltd, St Ives plc

Contents

Introduction

WordPerfect is considered to be one of the most popular word processing packages currently available for personal computer systems. Its sophisticated features allow you to do everything you could do with your typewriter and much more.

This Training Guide is designed to take you through a range of word processing features, introducing a complete package of documents used by a travel agency.

Requirements

It is certainly preferable to have a computer with a hard disk although WordPerfect will run on a computer with 2 floppy disk drives as long as the disk capacity is greater than 360K.

WordPerfect requires at least 384K of RAM and between 2.5 and 4.5 Mb of available disk space.

The version of DOS installed on your computer must be 2.1 or later.

Conventions

Commands are typed in capitals e.g. SELECT, TYPE, SAVE.

Text to be typed is in bold type e.g. TYPE **WP**.

Menu options are in bold type e.g. SELECT the **Date text** option.

New terms are in italics e.g. *mail merge*.

Function keys are indicated by the function key number in a black box e.g. `F1`.

Key names separated by `+` means that you must press and hold down the first key whilst pressing the second key e.g. `CTRL + HOME`.

Key names separated by a space mean press the first key and release and then press the second key e.g. `HOME` `PGUP`.

The Enter or Return key (the large arrow key on the right of the standard keyboard) is indicated by the symbol `ENTER`.

Getting started

This guide assumes that WordPerfect is installed on your hard disk in a subdirectory called WP51. To load WordPerfect type in the following from the DOS C: prompt:

CD\WP51

WP

You will need to press the `ENTER` key after typing each of the above instructions.

WordPerfect will be loaded and you will see a screen which is blank apart from information regarding the page number and cursor position in the bottom right-hand corner.

Unless you specify otherwise, documents will be saved to the sub-directory WP51, the sub-directory holding the program files. This is where WordPerfect automatically saves documents if you have not changed the settings. You may find that your copy of WordPerfect has been set up to save your documents to a different sub-directory so that it is easier to copy them, en masse, to floppy diskette. If this is not the case, it is advisable to follow the instructions below to create a new sub-directory on your hard disk to save the documents to. If you prefer, you could save all documents to a floppy disk. This is referred to as saving documents to the A drive. The following instructions will give both alternatives.

We shall also change the settings within WordPerfect so that our documents are automatically saved to the new sub-directory or to the floppy disk. This is referred to as changing the defaults.

Loading WP

TURN on your machine and make sure that you are at the DOS prompt. The screen should display C:\ (or something similar).

TYPE **CD\WP51** and PRESS `ENTER` to change directory to the sub-directory holding the WordPerfect program files.

TYPE **WP** and PRESS `ENTER` to load WordPerfect.

Data Directory

If you intend to save the documents on the hard disk, you should create a new sub-directory. To do this, first PRESS `F5`.

You will see a list of the files in the current data sub-directory. Unless the defaults have been changed on your machine this will be the WP51 sub-directory as displayed in the following illustration:

```
02-12-91  10:33p              Directory C:\WP51\*.*
Document size:          0    Free: 15,261,696 Used:  4,077,027    Files:    114

.    CURRENT   <DIR>                  ..    PARENT   <DIR>
LEARN    .       <DIR>  31-07-91 10:23p  8514A    .VRS   4,860  06-09-90 02:52p
ALTL     .WPM      121  02-07-91 03:12a  ALTN     .WPM     212  02-07-91 03:27a
ALTRNAT  .WPK      919  06-09-90 03:00p  ALTS     .WPM      79  02-07-91 03:15a
APPEAR   .PRN    1,021  24-06-91 04:21a  ARROW-22.WPG      187  06-09-90 02:52p
ATI      .VRS   12,851  06-09-90 02:52p  BALLOONS.WPG   3,187  06-09-90 02:52p
BANNER-3.WPG      719  06-09-90 02:52p  BICYCLE  .WPG     607  06-09-90 02:52p
BKGRND-1.WPG   11,391  06-09-90 02:52p  BORDER-8.WPG     215  06-09-90 02:52p
BULB     .WPG    2,101  06-09-90 02:52p  BURST-1  .WPG     819  06-09-90 02:52p
BUTTRFLY.WPG    5,349  06-09-90 02:52p  CALC     .WPM   7,972  06-09-90 03:00p
CALENDAR.WPG      371  06-09-90 02:52p  CERTIF   .WPG     679  06-09-90 02:52p
CHARACTR.DOC   46,799  06-09-90 03:00p  CHARMAP  .TST  42,644  06-09-90 02:52p
CHKBOX-1.WPG      653  06-09-90 02:52p  CLOCK    .WPG   1,811  06-09-90 02:52p
CNTRCT-2.WPG    2,753  06-09-90 02:52p  CODES    .WPM   7,403  06-09-90 03:00p
CONVERT  .EXE  109,229  06-09-90 03:00p  CURSOR   .COM   1,452  06-09-90 03:00p
DEVICE-2.WPG      657  06-09-90 02:52p  DIPLOMA  .WPG   2,413  06-09-90 02:52p
EGA512   .FRS    3,584  06-09-90 02:52p  EGAITAL  .FRS   3,584  06-09-90 02:52p
EGASMC   .FRS    3,584  06-09-90 02:52p  EGAUND   .FRS   3,584  06-09-90 02:52p
EHANDLER.PS     2,797  22-06-90 10:42a ▼ ENDFOOT  .WPM   3,953  06-09-90 03:00p

1 Retrieve; 2 Delete; 3 Move/Rename; 4 Print; 5 Short/Long Display;
6 Look; 7 Other Directory; 8 Copy; 9 Find; N Name Search: 6
```

To create a new sub-directory TYPE **7** or **O** to select the **Other directory** option.

At the bottom of the screen you will see the prompt "New directory = C:\WP51". The cursor
will be flashing under the letter C. USE the [Û→] to move to the end of the prompt (after the 1)
and TYPE **\DATA** , so that the whole directory path reads: C:\WP51\DATA.
PRESS [ENTER] to confirm.

The following prompt will appear:

```
Create C:\WP51\DATA? No (Yes)
```

TYPE **Y** to select the **Yes** option.

PRESS [F7] to exit from the **List files** screen.

We have now created a sub-directory called DATA which is, for those familiar with DOS, one
level below the WP51 sub-directory in the directory tree.

Change Defaults

The next step is to change the WordPerfect defaults so that our documents are automatically saved to either the new sub-directory or to the A drive.

PRESS `SHIFT + F1` to access the **Setup** options.

```
Setup

    1 - Mouse

    2 - Display

    3 - Environment

    4 - Initial Settings

    5 - Keyboard Layout

    6 - Location of Files
```

SELECT the **Location of files** option by typing **6** or **L**. The following screen will appear:

```
Setup: Location of Files

    1 - Backup Files

    2 - Keyboard/Macro Files          C:\WP51

    3 - Thesaurus/Spell/Hyphenation
                        Main
                        Supplementary

    4 - Printer Files                 C:\WP51

    5 - Style Files
               Library Filename

    6 - Graphic Files                 C:\WP51

    7 - Documents

    8 - Spreadsheet Files
```

We need to tell WordPerfect where we want to save our documents. TYPE **7** or **D** to select the **Documents** option. Either TYPE **C:\WP51\DATA** to save documents to the new sub-directory, or TYPE **A:** to save documents to floppy disk. PRESS `ENTER` to confirm.

PRESS `F7` to exit.

Section A: The basic process ▆▆▆▆▆▆▆▆▆

Task 1   Creating, saving and printing a document

Objective   To create a simple letter, save it to disk and produce a printed copy.

Instructions   Load WordPerfect as outlined in the Getting Started section of this guide.

Typing in text with WordPerfect is very similar to using a typewriter. The only thing you have to remember is not to press **ENTER** at the end of each line. Only press **ENTER** when you need to force a new line e.g. for headings and at the end of paragraphs. In other instances, WordPerfect will automatically wrap the text between the set margins. This is known as wordwrap.

Activity 1.1   Creating a document

TYPE in the following text pressing the **ENTER** key where indicated by the ↵ symbol.

Do not worry about any typing errors at this stage. We will look at the methods available for correcting text in a later activity.

Mrs Jane Cooper ↵
10 The Avenue ↵
Leeds LS6 8YT ↵
↵
↵
Dear Mrs Cooper ↵
↵
Thank you for your recent enquiry regarding holidays to Australia and New Zealand. ↵
↵
I have enclosed copies of all current brochures with details of available stop-overs in Singapore, Thailand and Malaysia. I will forward any additional brochures as soon as we receive them. ↵
↵
If I can provide any further information do not hesitate to call. ↵
↵
Yours sincerely ↵
↵
↵
Samantha King ↵
Travel Consultant ↵

The text that you have just typed is stored in the computer's memory. This is not a permanent storage location as it is *wiped clean* when you leave WordPerfect or when you start to work on a new document. To save a document permanently so that it can be accessed later, you must save the document to disk. Documents can be saved to your computer's *hard disk* or to a *floppy diskette*.

When you save a document, you will be prompted to give your new document a name. The name you choose should be easily identifiable and must be no more than 8 characters in length. An optional 3 characters can be added to the filename separated by a period (.). This is referred to as an extension. Do not use spaces and punctuation symbols in file names other than hyphens (-), underscores ( ) and the single period (.) used to separate the file name from the extension.

Examples:

The following document names are acceptable:

> LETTER
> LETTER.WP
> DRAFT.DOC
> MEMO2
> MEMO_12.WP

The following document names are not acceptable:

> MEMO 2.WP   spaces are not allowed
> LETTER_12A   too many letters
> DRAFT.*   the * cannot be used in document names

Activity 1.2   Saving a document

It is always advisable to save a document before printing. To save your document PRESS `F10`.

At the prompt "Document to be saved:" TYPE **COOPER.**

The document will be saved in the C:\WP51\DATA subdirectory (or the A drive if you selected this as the default).

Activity 1.3   Printing a document

To print your letter switch on the printer and then PRESS `SHIFT + F7`.

```
Print

        1 - Full Document
        2 - Page
        3 - Document on Disk
        4 - Control Printer
        5 - Multiple Pages
        6 - View Document
        7 - Initialise Printer


Options

        S - Select Printer             HP LaserJet III PostScri
        B - Binding Offset             0"
        N - Number of Copies           1
        U - Multiple Copies Generated by   WordPerfect
        G - Graphics Quality           Medium
        T - Text Quality               High
```

Various options are available. For the moment, SELECT the **Full document** option by TYPING **F** or **1**. The full document will be printed out.

Activity 1.4   Creating a new document

In order to create a new document we need to clear the current document from the computer's memory. As we have already saved our current document we can safely do this.

PRESS **F7**. You will be prompted to save the current document. As we have already saved it, we can TYPE **N** to select the **No** option.

You will now be asked if you want to exit WordPerfect. TYPE **N** to select the **No** option. You are presented with a clear screen so that you can create a new document.

TYPE the text outlined in the following example remembering to press the **ENTER** key only when you need to force a new line.

```
Sun Travel Holidays International
121 High Street
London WC2 6TY


Dear Sir

With reference to my recent letter dated 5th May, I have still
not received any brochures for holiday destinations in
Australasia or Asia.

The brochures for Europe arrived over 2 weeks ago and I am
concerned that the remaining brochures may have gone astray in
the post.

I would be most grateful if you could look into this matter as
I have several clients interested in travelling to Australia and
New Zealand later this year who are understandably becoming
frustrated waiting for these brochures to arrive.

I look forward to hearing from you by return of post.

Yours faithfully
```

SAVE this document as **SUN**.

PRINT the document.

REMOVE the document from the computer's memory.

Activity 1.5   Exiting from WordPerfect

To end a WordPerfect session PRESS **F7**. If you have a document currently on screen, you will be prompted to save that document before exiting. SELECT **Yes** to save and **No** to exit without saving.

You are then offered the option, "Exit WP (Y/N)?". SELECT **Yes** to exit from WordPerfect.

Key words   **Wordwrap**
Save
Filename
Extension

Task 2   Using the menus, mouse and help facility

Objective   To find our way around the WordPerfect *menus* and *help screens* using the *mouse* and keyboard.

Instructions   There are several ways in which you can *interact* with WordPerfect. We have already seen that we can use the function keys to tell WordPerfect what to do; for example, to save or print a document. With practice, it becomes easier to remember which key combinations to press for each command. You may prefer, however, to select these commands from a menu. You can then move through the menus to find the option you want. This is much easier than having to remember the key combinations but it can also be much slower.

You will probably find, as you progress with Wordperfect, that you use the key combinations for the commands you use regularly, and the menus for commands you use less frequently. If you have a mouse attached to your machine you can speed up the selection from menus considerably as we will see in a later activity.

Up until now, we have used the *function keys* to call up WordPerfect commands. For example, to print a document we pressed `SHIFT + F7`. Throughout the remainder of this text, commands will be accessed by function keys; it is generally found by existing WordPerfect users, that the keyboard method provides greater productivity. You may prefer, however, to use a combination of methods, as outlined in this task.

Menus - The WordPerfect commands can also be accessed via a *menu* system.

The WordPerfect menu can be accessed by pressing `ALT + =`. Menu options can be selected by moving the cursor to the required option and pressing the `ENTER` key. Alternatively, the menus can be selected by pressing the highlighted letter in the option name (usually the first letter). Sub-menus can be selected in a similar way. To move backwards through the menus, press `F1` or `ESCAPE` as many times as necessary to get you back to the required menu.

To exit the menus in one step, press `F7`, the exit key.

Mouse - Another method of selecting menu options is to use a mouse.

A mouse is a small hand-held device that allows you to interact with the WordPerfect menus. A mouse is entirely optional but can be a useful tool for moving quickly around the menus. In addition to selecting menus, the mouse can also be used for scrolling through the document to position the cursor before typing. It can also be used to mark blocks of text that are to be moved, copied or deleted. This will be looked at in a later task.

If you have a mouse, you can turn the menu bar on and off by *clicking* (pressing once) the right mouse button. Menu options can be selected by pointing to the option with the mouse, and clicking the left mouse button. To back out of the menus, click the right mouse button..

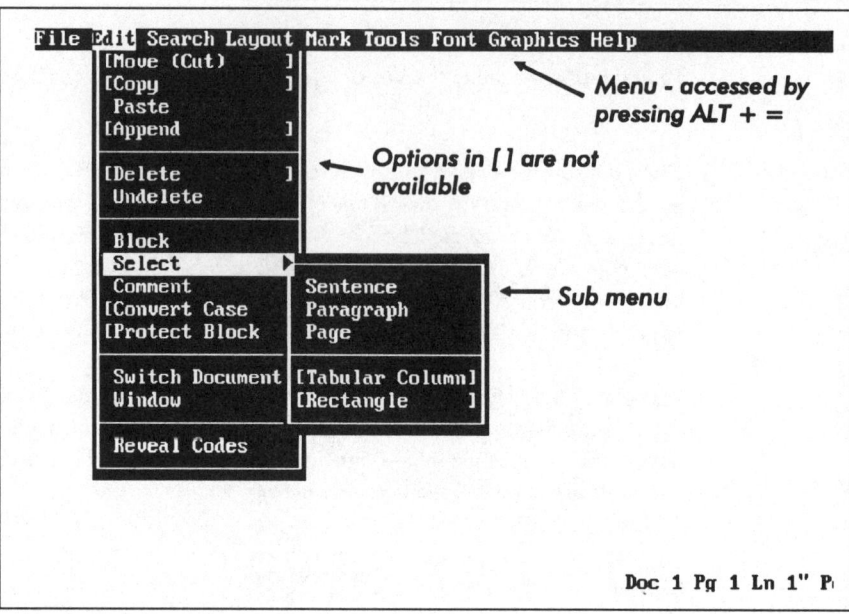

File **Edit** Search Layout Mark Tools Font Graphics Help

```
[Move (Cut)      ]
[Copy            ]
 Paste
[Append          ]

[Delete          ]
 Undelete

 Block
 Select           ▶      Sentence
 Comment                 Paragraph
[Convert Case            Page
[Protect Block

 Switch Document [Tabular Column]
 Window          [Rectangle     ]

 Reveal Codes
```

Menu - accessed by pressing ALT + =

Options in [ ] are not available

Sub menu

Doc 1 Pg 1 Ln 1" P

Activity 2.1   Retrieving and printing a document

In this activity we will use the menus to retrieve and print our document. The term *retrieve* means to copy a document from disk to the computer's memory where it can be changed.

LOAD WordPerfect as outlined in the Getting Started section.

CALL UP the menus by PRESSING `ALT + =`.

SELECT the **File menu** by TYPING **F** or HIGHLIGHTING the word **File** and PRESSING the `ENTER` key.

SELECT the menu option **Retrieve**. You can do this by either TYPING **R** or by simply PRESSING `ENTER` as the **Retrieve** option is the first in the list and already highlighted.

At this stage you can type the name of the document you want to retrieve. If you are unsure of the name of the document you can ask WordPerfect to show you a list of documents in the area of your disk where the files are saved. This is termed a *sub-directory*.

PRESS `F5` for a list.

The sub-directory name is displayed as C:\WP51*.* or A:\ depending on how you set up the defaults in the Getting Started section.

PRESS `ENTER` to confirm the location of your documents.

HIGHLIGHT the document **COOPER** and TYPE **R** or **1** to retrieve the document.

CALL UP the menus again, and SELECT the **File menu** and **Print** option. TYPE **F** or **1** to print the full document.

Activity 2.2

Using the mouse

If you have a mouse attached to your machine which is installed correctly for WordPerfect, you should be able to slide the mouse across your desk and see the mouse pointer move on the screen. The mouse pointer will move in the same direction that you slide the mouse.

CLICK the **Right** mouse button to display the menu.

SLIDE the mouse so that the mouse pointer is pointing to the **File menu** option.

CLICK the **Left** mouse button to display the **File menu**.

MOVE the mouse pointer to the **Print** option. CLICK the **Left** mouse button.

We do not want to print our document at the moment so we will CLICK the **Right** mouse button to come out of the menus. You will need to click the right button once for each level of the menus.

Instructions

WordPerfect's *help system* is designed to be context sensitive. This means that the help given is relevant to what you are doing at the time. For example, if you are retrieving a file and request help, you will be given help information on the **File Retrieve** options. **Help** can be accessed at any time by pressing ▨. If you ask for help while typing or editing a document you will be shown the help information screen:

```
Help            Licence Number:              WP 5.1


    Press any letter to get an alphabetical list of features.

        The list will include the features that start with that letter,
        along with the name of the key where the feature can be found.
        You can then press that key to get a description of how the
        feature works.


    Press any function key to get information about the use of the key.

        Some keys may enable you to choose from a menu to get information
        about various options.  Press HELP again to display the template.
```

When presented with the *help information* screen, press the first letter of the topic name to get help on a specific topic. To get further help, press the key combination displayed in the right hand column.

Activity 2.3

Using help

Exit the menus and PRESS `F3` to access **Help**. To get help on the block command TYPE **B** (we will be using this command in the next task).

```
Features [B]                            WordPerfect Key      Keystrokes

Backspace (Erase)                       Backspace            Backspace
Backup Directory Location               Setup                Shft-F1,6
Backup Files, Automatic                 Setup                Shft-F1,3,1,1
Backup Options                          Setup                Shft-F1,3,1
Backward Search                         <-Search             Shft-F2
Base Font                               Font                 Ctrl-F8,4
Base Font (Document)                    Format               Shft-F8,3,3
Base Font (Printer)                     Print                Shft-F7,s,3,5
Baseline Placement for Typesetters      Format               Shft-F8,4,6,5
Beep Options                            Setup                Shft-F1,3,2
Binding Offset                          Print                Shft-F7,b
Binding Offset (Default)                Setup                Shft-F1,4,8,1
Black and White, View Document In       Setup                Shft-F1,2,5,1
Block                                   Block                Alt-F4
Block, (Assign Variable w/Block On)     Macro Commands       Ctrl-PgUp
Block, Append (Block On)                Move                 Ctrl-F4,1,4
Block, Centre (Block On)                Centre               Shft-F6
Block, Comment (Block On)               Text In/Out          Ctrl-F5
```

To get more help on the block command, PRESS the keys in the right-hand column, `ALT + F4`.

```
Block On/Off

        Defines a block of text on which various operations may be performed. The
        block will be highlighted as it is defined.

To define a block:

    1  Position the cursor at the beginning or end of the block of text.
    2  Press Block (Alt-F4).
    3  Move the cursor to the opposite end of the block.  Use the arrow keys, or
       type a character to advance to that character.  You can also use Search->
       or <-Search to move the highlighting to the character(s) entered here.

You may then use the following features:
        Append    - Press Move to append the block to the end of a file.
        Bold      - Embolden the highlighted text.
        Comment   - Press Text In/Out to change text to a comment.
        Underline - Underline text.
        Centre    - Centre blocked lines.
        Delete    - Press Del or Backspace to delete the block.
        Flush Rgt - Move blocked lines to right margin.
        Font      - Change the appearance or size of printed text.
        Type 1 for more...

Selection: 0                                    (Press ENTER to exit Help)
```

TYPE **1** to get more information on the **Block** command.

EXIT the Help screens by PRESSING `ENTER`.

To get help on the function keys PRESS `F3` twice. PRESS `ENTER` to exit. A full list of the function keys can be found in Appendix 2.

Activity 2.4   Practice

Experiment further with the help facilities. Use the help index to find out more about the **Print** and **Retrieve** commands. Use the function key `F3` help to determine the keyboard shortcut for the **Retrieve** command.

Key words   **Menu**
            Retrieve
            Help
            Context Sensitive

Section B: Text manipulation

One of the main advantages a word processor has over a typewriter is the fact that text can be easily changed. The text is held in the computer's memory and displayed on the screen. The changing of this text is referred to as *editing*. Although most modern typewriters hold a line or two of text in memory so some changes can be made, it is certainly much easier to edit text using a word processor.

Task 3 — Moving around and editing a document

Objective

This task will look at keyboard shortcuts for moving around a document and ways to make changes to an existing document by adding and deleting text.

Instructions

Moving around - In addition to the four arrow, or cursor, keys ($\leftarrow \uparrow \rightarrow \downarrow$) there are a number of keyboard shortcuts for moving around your document. For a summary of these, refer to Appendix 1.

Inserting text - By default, WordPerfect is in insert mode. If you move your cursor to the position where you want to add text, you can simply start typing. The text will automatically be inserted.

Overtyping text - The Insert key (INS on some keyboards) acts as a *toggle* between insert and overtype modes. Press it once and you can overtype existing text. Press it again and you are back to insert mode.

Deleting Text - The easiest ways to delete text is to use either the Backspace key to delete characters to the left of the cursor, or the Delete key to delete characters at the cursor position. There are a range of other deleting shortcuts which are listed in Appendix 1.

Activity 3.1

Editing text

CLEAR the screen by PRESSING **F7** and TYPING **N** twice in response to the prompts.

PRESS **SHIFT + F10** to retrieve a file. TYPE **SUN** as the document name and PRESS **ENTER** to confirm.

The letter you created in the previous activity is loaded into the computer's memory. We can now make changes to the letter.

[Refer to the example on the following page]

USE the **↓** key to move to the beginning of the first line of the first paragraph.

PRESS `CTRL + →` to move across a word at a time, to the word "May". PRESS `→` 3 times to move the cursor to the ",". TYPE `SPACE` **1992** . The text 1992 will be inserted at the cursor position.

Sun Travel Holidays International
121 High Street
London WC2 6TY

1992

Dear Sir

With reference to my recent letter dated 5th May, I have still not received any brochures for holiday destinations in Australasia or Asia.

and America

The brochures for Europe arrived over 2 weeks ago and I am concerned that the remaining brochures may have gone astray in the post.

give *your immediate attention*

I would be most grateful if you could ~~look into~~ this matter as I have several clients interested in travelling to Australia and New Zealand later this year who are understandably becoming frustrated waiting for these brochures to arrive.

I look forward to hearing from you by return of post.

Yours faithfully *Please telephone me on (0532) 64172 as soon as you have any information.*

MOVE the cursor to the space following the word "Europe" on the first line of the second paragraph and INSERT **and America** .

MOVE to the word "look" in the first line of the third paragraph and PRESS `CTRL + BACKSPACE` to delete the whole word.

DELETE the following word, "into", in the same way. TYPE **give** in their place.

MOVE further along the same line and INSERT the text **your immediate attention** before the word "as".

MOVE to the beginning of the last paragraph "I look forward..." and PRESS `CTRL + END` to delete the whole line.

TYPE **Please telephone me on (0532) 64172 as soon as you have any information** to replace this text.

SAVE this document replacing the current version on disk.

Activity 3.2   Using the system date and more editing practice

CLEAR the screen and RETRIEVE the document **COOPER** that we created earlier. Either use the keyboard shortcut, `SHIFT + F10`, or SELECT the **File** and **Retrieve** options from the menu. When prompted for the name of the document TYPE **COOPER** and PRESS the `ENTER` key.

WordPerfect has an inbuilt feature for adding the system date to a document.

MOVE to a blank line between the address and the start of the letter and PRESS `SHIFT + F5`.

A menu will appear at the bottom of the screen. SELECT **Date text** by TYPING **T** or **1** or SELECT **Date code** by TYPING **C** or **2** (with **Date text** the current date is entered as text whereas with **Date code**, the date will change to the current date whenever the document is retrieved).

PRACTICE moving around the document using the keyboard shortcuts listed in Appendix 1.

USE the editing keys to make the changes outlined in the following example.

Mrs Jane Cooper
10 The Avenue
Leeds LS6 8YT
West Yorkshire   *Add todays date*

Dear Mrs Cooper,

Thank you for your recent enquiry regarding holidays to Australia
and New Zealand.   *Hong Kong*

I have enclosed copies of all current brochures with details of
available stop overs in ~~Singapore~~, Thailand and Malaysia. I will
forward any additional brochures as soon as we receive them.

If I can provide any further information do not hesitate to call.

Yours sincerely,
                              My direct number is 64172.

Samantha King
Travel Consultant

When you have completed the changes, SAVE and PRINT your document.

Keywords   Insert
Overtype
Date text
Date Code

Task 4 Working with blocks of text

Objective

To add text attributes, such as *bold* and *underlining*, and to change the position of blocks of text.

Instructions

Text can be *formatted* as it is typed or it can be formatted afterwards. This activity will look at changing the positioning and attributes of text after it has been typed. To do this, text must be *blocked*. A block of text is simply a group of letters or words. To highlight a group, *either*, position your cursor on the first letter of the group, press `ALT + F4` and use the `→` key to highlight the block; or, move the mouse pointer to the beginning of the block, hold down the left mouse button and *drag* the mouse so that the block is highlighted. Release the mouse button.

Once highlighted, press the appropriate keys for the format required: e.g. `F6` to change the text to bold.

Text can also be blocked by pressing `ALT + F4` followed by a cursor movement shortcut key. For example, by pressing `ALT + F4` followed by `HOME` `HOME` `↓`, the text will be blocked from the current cursor position to the end of the document.

In the following activities the instructions will involve blocking the text using the function keys. If you have a mouse attached, you can use the mouse instead.

Activity 4.1

Changing text using block commands

ERASE the current document from the screen by PRESSING `F7` to exit. When prompted to save the document TYPE **N** for **No** (unless you haven't previously saved the current document). When asked "Exit WP?" TYPE **N** for No. A blank screen should appear allowing you to enter a new document.

TYPE in the text as it appears in the next example. SAVE the document as **MEMO**.

```
Down Under Holidays

Memo

To:  Sally Prim, Melbourne Office

From: Samantha King, Leeds Office       Use the inbuilt date
                                        feature to enter today's
13 June 1992  ←                         date

The above clients will be arriving on flight SI25J on Monday 5th
August at 9.30 a.m.  Please arrange for the courier to meet them
at the airport and take them to their first destination.
```

BLOCK the text "Down Under Holidays" by moving to the D of Down, PRESSING `ALT + F4` and then PRESSING the `END` key to HIGHLIGHT the whole line.

To CENTRE this blocked text, PRESS `SHIFT + F6`. Use the same steps to CENTRE the word "Memo".

BLOCK the 2 lines of text that are now centred and PRESS `SHIFT + F3` to change the text to upper case. When prompted, SELECT the **Uppercase** option.

BLOCK the date and the blank line directly below. PRESS `CTRL + F4` to move the block. SELECT **Block** by TYPING **B** or **1**. SELECT **Move** by TYPING **M** or **1**. The highlighted block will disappear. MOVE the cursor to above the line "To: Sally....." and PRESS the `ENTER` key. The block will reappear in the new position.

INSERT the line **Re: Holiday itinerary for Mr & Mrs Cooper** as shown below.

MOVE the cursor to the blank line above the text "The above clients...". We will insert a dividing line using the repeat key as a shortcut. PRESS `ESCAPE` and TYPE **64**, and then PRESS `=`. The (=) character will be repeated 64 times between the current margins.

BLOCK the flight number S125J. To make this information stand out, *either* PRESS `F6` to **Bold** or `F8` to **Underline** the blocked text. Use the same procedure to bold the text "To:", "From:" and "Re:".

Your document should now resemble the following example. SAVE your document using the same name and replacing the current version on disk.

```
                      DOWN UNDER HOLIDAYS

                             MEMO



     13 June 1992

     To:  Sally Prim, Melbourne Office

     From: Samantha King, Leeds Office

     Re:  Holiday itinerary for Mr & Mrs Cooper


     ================================================================

     The above clients will be arriving on flight S125J on Monday 5th
     August at 9.30 a.m.  Please arrange for the courier to meet them
     at the airport and take them to their first destination.
```

Practice

CLEAR the screen and RETRIEVE the document **SUN**.

BLOCK the address and change it to uppercase.

INSERT a reference and underline it.

BOLD the telephone number in the last paragraph.

```
SUN TRAVEL HOLIDAYS INTERNATIONAL  ◄
121 HIGH STREET                          Uppercase
LONDON WC2 6TY          ◄


Our Reference: SK12/6.4    ◄──── Underlined

Dear Sir

With reference to my recent letter dated 5th May 1992, I have
still not received any brochures for holiday destinations in
Australasia or Asia.

The brochures for Europe and America arrived over 2 weeks ago and
I am concerned that the remaining brochures may have gone astray
in the post.

I would be most grateful if you could give this matter your
immediate attention as I have several clients interested in
travelling to Australia and New Zealand later this year who are
understandably becoming frustrated waiting for these brochures
to arrive.

Please telephone me on (0532) 64172 as soon as you have any
                    ◄──── Bold
```

SAVE your changes.

Key words	Block
	Text Attribute

Task 5

Working with tabs and codes

Objective

To use *tabs* to position text, add *formatting codes* as we type and to remove unwanted formatting codes.

Instructions

WordPerfect *automatically* sets tab stops at every half inch, starting at the left margin. For the moment we will use these pre-set tab stops but in later activities we will see how to change them to suit our document style. To move the cursor to the first tab stop press the `TAB` key (usually situated to the left of the keyboard above the `CAPS LOCK` key). Press the `TAB` key again to move to the second tab stop and so on.

Activity 5.1

Using tabs

CLEAR the screen and RETRIEVE the document **MEMO**.

INSERT a tab between "To:" and "Sally Prim...." by moving the cursor to the S of Sally and PRESSING the `TAB` key. In the same way, INSERT a tab before "Samantha..." and before "Holiday itinerary...".

POSITION the cursor at the end of the document and PRESS the `ENTER` key twice.

PRESS the `TAB` key to position the cursor at the next tab stop. PRESS `F6` to turn **Bold** on. TYPE the text **Monday 5th:**. PRESS `F6` again to turn **Bold** off.

PRESS the `TAB` key again to position the cursor at the next tab stop. TYPE the text **The Holiday Inn - City**.

COMPLETE the document as indicated below, TYPING the day information in bold. SAVE and REPLACE the document.

```
To:       Sally Prim, Melbourne Office

From:     Samantha King, Leeds Office

Re:       Holiday itinerary for Mr & Mrs Cooper

===============================================================

The above clients will be arriving on flight S125J on Monday 5th
August at 9.30 a.m.  Please arrange for the courier to meet them
at the airport and take them to their first destination.

        Monday 5th:     The Holiday Inn - City
        Tuesday 6th:    The Holiday Inn - City
        Wednesday 7th:  The Alexandra Hotel - Ballarat
        Thursday 8th:   Flight AN456 to Sydney

I have sent a memo to Jo in Sydney outlining the NSW itinerary.
```

16

The previous activity looked at how we can insert text attributes, such as bold, at the time of entering the text. The occasion will arise when you change your mind and want to remove the text attributes or positioning attributes you have added.

Every time you use the WordPerfect commands to change the way your text looks, a *code* is added to your document. When viewing or printing the document, these codes are invisible. In this activity we will see how to look at these codes and remove them. Codes can be *revealed* and *edited* by pressing `ALT + F3` or by pressing `F11` if this key is available on your keyboard.

Activity 5.2

Editing codes

PRESS `ALT + F3` or `F11` to show the codes. MOVE the cursor to the formatting code before the flight number, this may be bold or underline depending on which attribute you chose, and PRESS the `DELETE` key to remove the code.

HIDE the codes again by PRESSING `ALT + F3` or `F11`.

```
To:        Sally Prim, Melbourne Office

From:      Samantha King, Leeds Office

Re:        Holiday itinerary for Mr & Mrs Cooper

=============================================================

The above clients will be arriving on flight SI25J on Monday 5th
C:\WP51\MEMO.WP                           Doc 1 Pg 1 Ln 3.5" Pos 5.5"
{  ▲    ▲    ▲    ▲    ▲    ▲    ▲    ▲   /▲    ▲    ▲ ] ▲    ▲    ▲
[HRt]
===============================================================[HRt]
[HRt]
The above clients will be arriving on flight [UND]SI25J[und] on Monday 5th[SRt]
August at 9.30 a.m.  Please arrange for the courier to meet them[SRt]
at the airport and take them to their first destination.[HRt]
[HRt]
[Tab][BOLD]Monday 5th:[bold][Tab]The Holiday Inn [-] City[HRt]
[Tab][BOLD]Tuesday 6th:[bold][Tab]The Holiday Inn [-] City[HRt]
[Tab][BOLD]Wednesday 7th:[bold][Tab]The Alexandra Hotel [-] Ballarat[HRt]

Press Reveal Codes to restore screen
```

SAVE your document in the usual way.

Key words   Tab
Formatting Code

Task 6   Customising tabs

Objective

To produce a travel itinerary and covering letter, introducing *flush right alignment*, *forced page breaks* and *customised tab settings*.

Instructions

If you are typing letters without headed paper, you may want to align your address block to the right of the page. We have already seen how to centre and move a block of text. The same blocking method is required for flush right alignment. Type the text to be aligned, select the text using `ALT + F4`, and press `ALT + F6` to position the block flush right. Select **Yes** to move the block.

Activity 6.1   Flush right alignment

CLEAR the screen ready for a new document and TYPE the following letter. TYPE the address to the left, BLOCK it and PRESS `ALT + F6` to give flush right alignment. Position the date in the same way. Use the `TAB` key to INDENT the first line of the paragraph. SAVE as **COOPER2**.

```
                                          Down Under Holidays
                                             21 High Street
                                             Leeds LS1 4RT

Mr & Mrs Cooper
10 The Avenue
Leeds LS6 8YT

                                             20 June 1992

Dear Mr & Mrs Cooper


    Please find enclosed a copy of your holiday itinerary as
discussed in our telephone conversation last week. If you would
like to make any changes please telephone, or come into the
office next time you are passing.

Regards


Samantha King
```

So far, our documents have all been short, taking up less than a page. With longer documents, WordPerfect will automatically produce a new page when needed. This is referred to as an *automatic page break*. Sometimes, it is necessary to *force* a page break if you want your document to continue on the next page but you have not filled the current page. To force a new page, simply position your cursor at the end of the text on the current page and press `CTRL + ENTER`.

Activity 6.2

Adding a forced page break

MOVE your cursor to the end of your letter COOPER2 and PRESS `CTRL + ENTER`. A dashed line will appear across the page indicating a page break.

Instructions

As we have already seen, WordPerfect has tab stops at every half inch. These tab stops are *left aligned*, meaning that characters typed at the tab position will appear to the left of the tab stop. You can change both the spacing between tabs and the type of tab.

Left Aligned - The default tab type, characters appear to the left of the tab stop.

Right Aligned - Characters appear to the right of the tab stop, giving a flush right alignment. Could be used for columns of numbers without decimal places.

Centre Aligned - Characters are centred around the tab stop.

Decimal Aligned - The decimal point is aligned at the tab stop. Suitable for columns of numbers with decimal places.

To change the tab settings, first position your cursor at the beginning of the line where you want the new settings to take effect. Any changes you make will affect all text from this point to the end of the document or, to the next tab change. Press `SHIFT + F8` and select **Line** followed by **Tab set** from the menus. The current tab settings appear at the bottom of the screen and can be changed using the usual editing keys. The following activity will involve changing the spacing and type of tab stops.

Activity 6.3

Deleting pre-set tab stops

MOVE your cursor to below the page-break line in COOPER2. TYPE the following, PRESSING the `ENTER` key at the end of each line:

**Holiday Itinerary For Mr & Mrs Cooper
2nd - 26th August 1991**

CENTRE these 2 lines of text. Leave 2 blank lines and TYPE:

`TAB` **August**

Leave another blank line and TYPE:

`TAB` **2nd** `TAB` **Leave Manchester 9.30 a.m.**

Leave another blank line and TYPE:

`TAB` **3rd-4th** `TAB` **Singapore**

Due to the half-inch tab stops, the text is not aligning very well. To solve this problem we could insert 2 tab stops between the date and place. A more tidy method is to change the tab stops. Position your cursor either above or at the beginning of the line that starts "2nd..". PRESS `SHIFT + F8`. SELECT **Line.** SELECT **Tab set.** Your screen should look similar to the following:

```
Samantha King

=======================================================================
                 Holiday Itinerary for Mr & Mrs Cooper
                         2nd - 26th August 1991


        August

        2nd  Leave Manchester 9.30 a.m.
        3rd-4th    Singapore



L....L...L...L...L...L...L...L...L...L...L...L...L....L.
:    ^    :    ^    :    ^    :    ^    :    ^    :    ^
0"        +1"       +2"       +3"       +4"       +5"       +6"
Delete EOL (clear tabs); Enter Number (set tab); Del (clear tab);
Type; Left; Centre; Right; Decimal; .= Dot Leader; Press Exit when
```

Use the `→` key to move to the left tab stop (L) at the 1" mark. PRESS `DELETE` to delete this tab stop. The second tab stop is now at 1.5". To exit, PRESS `F7` twice.

TYPE the rest of the itinerary pressing the `TAB` key after the date:

```
        August

        2nd              Leave Manchester 9.30 a.m.
        3rd-4th          Singapore
        5th              Arrive Melbourne, Australia 9.30 a.m.
        6th              Melbourne
        7th              Ballarat
        8th-13th         Sydney
        14th-16th        Alice Springs/Ayres Rock
        17th-22nd        Cairns/Great Barrier Reef
        23rd-25th        Hong Kong
        26th             Arrive Manchester 7.20 p.m.
```

Leave 2 blank lines below the itinerary and TYPE:

TAB **Hotels**

Leave a blank line and TYPE:

TAB **Place** **TAB** **Hotel** **TAB** **Class** **TAB** **Price per Night**

POSITION the cursor at the beginning of the line you have just typed and use the steps covered in the previous activity to DELETE the tab stops as indicated in the following illustration:

```
        Hotels

        Place              Hotel              Class      Price per Night
L....L.................L..............L..............L.........L....L....L...L..
    ¦        ^       ¦        ^       ¦        ^       ¦        ^       ¦        ^       ¦        ^       ¦        ^
    0"              +1"              +2"              +3"              +4"              +5"              +6"
Delete EOL (clear tabs); Enter Number (set tab); Del (clear tab);
Type; Left; Centre; Right; Decimal; .= Dot Leader; Press Exit when do
```

Activity 6.4   Centre and Decimal tabs

Leave a blank line under the column headings and TYPE the following:

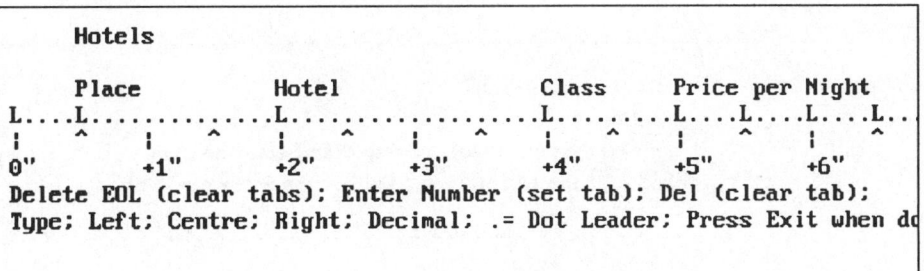

The last 2 columns would look better if we changed the alignment. MOVE the cursor to the left of the line that starts "Melbourne Holiday Inn.." and ENTER the command to change the tab formats. USE the **DELETE** key to remove the left tab at 4". TYPE a **C** at 1.2", to centre the **Class.** REMOVE the left tab at 5" and insert a decimal tab by TYPING **D** at 5.8". Exit by PRESSING **F7** twice.

```
        Place            Hotel              Class        Price per Night

        Melbourne        Holiday Inn        *****          $95.00
        Ballarat         Alexandra Hotel    ***            $55.00
        Sydney           Hyatt              *****          $120.00

L....L...............L.............................C...............D.L....L...
!      ^      !       ^     !        ^      !       ^     !        ^      !      ^
0"           +1"          +2"           +3"          +4"          +5"          +6"
Delete EOL (clear tabs); Enter Number (set tab); Del (clear tab);
Type; Left; Centre; Right; Decimal; .= Dot Leader; Press Exit when do
```

Instructions

It is as easy to indent an entire paragraph from the left margin as it is to indent the first line. To just indent the first line of the paragraph you press the **TAB** key before typing the text. To indent the entire paragraph you need to press **F4**, the **Indent** key, before typing the text.

Activity 6.5

Indenting a paragraph

Complete the hotel details as displayed below. Before typing the final paragraph, PRESS **F4**, the **Indent** key, to indent the entire paragraph to the first tab stop.

```
        Hotels

        Place            Hotel              Class        Price per Night

        Melbourne        Holiday Inn        *****          $95.00
        Ballarat         Alexandra Hotel    ***            $55.00
        Sydney           Hyatt              *****          $120.00
        Alice Springs    The Alice          ***            $85.00
        Cairns           Holiday Inn        *****          $95.00
        Hong Kong        Regent             ***            £40.00

        Please note, the accommodation for Singapore has not yet
        been finalised.  All prices are in Australian dollars apart
        from the Regent Hotel, Hong Kong which is priced in
        sterling.
```

22

Another type of popular indent is the *hanging* indent. With a hanging indent, the first line of the paragraph starts at the left margin and the rest of the paragraph is indented. This is a useful feature if you need to number paragraphs.

To create a hanging indent press `F4` the **Indent** key as many times as necessary to move the cursor to where you want the lines *beneath* the first line to be indented. Press `SHIFT + TAB` , the **Margin release** key to move the cursor back to the left margin. Type the paragraph, only pressing the `ENTER` key at the end of the paragraph. If you are typing numbers as the first characters in each paragraph, follow the instructions above but press the `TAB` key after the number (see following example).

Activity 6.6

Hanging indent

COMPLETE the document as displayed below.

Please note, the accommodation for Singapore has not yet been finalised. All prices are in Australian dollars apart from the Regent Hotel, Hong Kong which is priced in sterling.

Down Under Holidays would like to take this opportunity to inform you of our additional services, designed to make your holiday a pleasurable experience from start to finish.

1.   Our chauffeur driven limousine can collect you from home and take you to the airport. At the end of your holiday you will be met and driven back to your home.

2.   All excursions can be booked and paid for before your holiday.

3.   We can organise all forms of insurance. Telephone now for an appointment to discuss your requirements.

To create the hanging indents for the numbered paragraphs PRESS `F4` once then PRESS `SHIFT + TAB` to move the cursor back to the left margin. TYPE **1.** and then PRESS the `TAB` key. TYPE the rest of the paragraph pressing the `ENTER` key twice at the end to complete the paragraph and leave a blank line.

Follow the same procedure to enter points 2 and 3.

SAVE and PRINT the document.

Key words	Flush right
	Forced page break
	Tabs - Left, Right, Centre and Decimal
	Indent
	Hanging Indent

Task 7   Changing the size and appearance of text

Objective

To improve the appearance of the itinerary by changing the *appearance* and *size* of some of the text. It should be noted, at this stage, that the end result of this task is very much dependant on the capabilities of your printer. Not all printers are able to adjust the size and appearance of text. Completing this task will give you a good indication of your printer capabilities.

Instructions

The overall appearance of a document can easily be improved by giving some variety with text size and format. WordPerfect provides a range of text sizes:

```
You can change the size of text:

Fine

Small

Large

Very Large

Extra Large
```

The size of text can be changed by selecting a *block* in the usual way and then pressing
`CTRL + F8`, the **Font** key. Select the **Size** option followed by the required size. The text on the screen will be colour coded on a colour monitor. The actual sizes can be seen by accessing the print view screen. Press `SHIFT + F7` to call up the print menu and type
V for **View** to view your document on the screen.

The appearance of the text can be changed in a similar way.

```
You can change the appearance of tex

Bold                        Outline

Underlined                  Shadow

Double Undelined            SMALL CAPS

Italic                      Redline

Strikeout
```

Select the block to be changed and press `CTRL + F8`. Select the **Appearance** option and select the required format.

Size and appearance can also be changed before you type. Press `CTRL + F8` and select the required **Size** and/or **Appearance** formats. Type the text to be formatted and then press `CTRL + F8` again. Select the **Normal** option to turn all formatting off.

We shall use these new commands to improve the appearance of our itinerary:

Holiday Itinerary for Mr & Mrs Cooper
2nd - 26th August 1991

August

2nd	Leave Manchester 9.30 a.m.
3rd-4th	Singapore
5th	Arrive Melbourne, Australia 9.30 a.m.
6th	Melbourne
7th	Ballarat
8th-13th	Sydney
14th-16th	Alice Springs/Ayres Rock
17th-22nd	Cairns/Great Barrier Reef
23rd-25th	Hong Kong
26th	Arrive Manchester 7.20 p.m.

Hotels

Place	Hotel	Class	Price per Night
Melbourne	Holiday Inn	*****	$95.00
Ballarat	Alexandra Hotel	***	$55.00
Sydney	Hyatt	*****	$120.00
Alice Springs	The Alice	***	$85.00
Cairns	Holiday Inn	*****	$95.00
Hong Kong	Regent	***	£40.00

Activity 7.1

Changing the size of text

RETRIEVE the document **COOPER2** if it is not currently loaded.

MOVE to the second page and use the **Block** command, `ALT + F4`, or use the mouse to SELECT the heading "Holiday Itinerary for Mr & Mrs Cooper".

PRESS `CTRL + F8` to select the **Font** command. TYPE **1** or **S** to select the **Size** option. SELECT the **Very large** size option.

Repeat the above steps to change the size of the second heading "2nd - 26th August 1991" to **Large**. Also change the headings "August" and "Hotels" to **Large**.

PREVIEW your document by PRESSING `SHIFT + F7` and then TYPING **V** for **View**. When finished, PRESS `F7` to exit.

26

Activity 7.2	Changing the appearance of text

BLOCK the top title which is already colour coded for the **Very large** size format and PRESS `CTRL + F8`. TYPE **2** or **A** to select **Appearance**. SELECT the **Shadow** option.

Repeat the above steps to change the headings "August" and "Hotels" to **Bold** (there is a keyboard shortcut for Bold - can you remember it?). *F6*

Change the appearance of the table headings to **Double underline**. You can block the whole line: the spaces between the headings will not be underlined.

VIEW your document on the screen.

Activity 7.3	Changing the base font of a document

Again, this feature is very much determined by the capabilities of your printer. If your printer is capable of printing a range of fonts you can change the base font of your document in WordPerfect.

FONT

PRESS `CTRL + F8`. As you have not selected a block, there are extra features available, one of which is **Change base font**. If you select this option you will be presented with a list of available fonts. CHOOSE one of these and view your document to screen. Experiment with choosing different fonts. When you are happy with the appearance of your document, SAVE and PRINT.

Key words	**Size**
	Appearance
	Base Font

Section C: Graphics and templates

A couple of pictures or diagrams can turn simple text into an eye-catching document. On the other hand, however, too many pictures will take the reader's attention away from the text, thus defeating the object!

In this section we shall introduce the graphic features available with WordPerfect 5.1 and look at ways in which we can create a general template document that can be used as a starting point for future documents.

Task 8 — Incorporating text and graphic boxes

Objective

To include a banner heading for the travel itinerary incorporating WordPerfect *text* and *graphic boxes*.

Instructions

By adding 2 graphic boxes and 1 text box to our itinerary, we can improve the appearance substantially.

Down Under Holidays

Holiday Itinerary for Mr & Mrs Cooper

2nd - 26th August 1991

August

2nd	Leave Manchester 9.30 a.m.
3rd-4th	Singapore
5th	Arrive Melbourne, Australia 9.30 a.m.
6th	Melbourne
7th	Ballarat
8th-13th	Sydney
14th-16th	Alice Springs/Ayres Rock
17th-22nd	Cairns/Great Barrier Reef
23rd-25th	Hong Kong
26th	Arrive Manchester 7.20 p.m.

Hotels

WordPerfect offers four different types of boxes:

Figure Box - A box with a line around

Text Box - a shaded box with dark lines above and below

Table Box - the same as a Text Box but not shaded

User Box - like a Figure Box without the line around - a blank "hole"!

Although the names of the boxes give the impression that each type of box should hold different information, this is, in fact, not the case. Each kind of box can contain a picture, table, figure or text.

For this task we will use a text box to display the company name and user boxes to display the pictures.

Before creating a box you need to decide where the box is to be positioned. If the contents of the box are relevant to a particular paragraph in your document, the box can be attached to that paragraph. If you change the text in the paragraph, the box will "float" with the paragraph. If the box is to be used to hold a page heading, for example, it should be anchored to the page rather than a specific paragraph. The box will then remain with the page even if the text moves.

To create a box that is to be anchored to a paragraph, position your cursor on the first character of the paragraph.

To create a box that is to be anchored to a page, position your cursor at the top of the page or the top of the document.

Press `ALT + F9` to call up the **Graphics** options. Select the type of box you want to create. Select the **Create** option to create a new box.

Activity 8.1   Creating a User Box

RETRIEVE the document **COOPER2** and position your cursor at the top of the second page.

PRESS `ALT + F9` to access the **Graphics** options. TYPE **4** or **U** to SELECT the **User box**. TYPE **1** or **C** to **Create**. The following screen will appear:

```
Definition: User Box

     1 - Filename

     2 - Contents            Empty

     3 - Caption

     4 - Anchor Type         Paragraph

     5 - Vertical Position   0"

     6 - Horizontal Position Right

     7 - Size                3.13" wide x 3.13" (high)

     8 - Wrap Text Around Box Yes

     9 - Edit
```

Activity 8.2

Filling a user box with a graphic

TYPE **1** or **F** to SELECT **Filename**. PRESS `F5` for a list of files. The directory path C:\WP51*.* will be displayed. This is the directory containing the graphics files.

PRESS `HOME` `→` `BACKSPACE` to delete the last *. TYPE **WPG** and PRESS `ENTER`

You will be presented with the selection of graphics files that come with your WordPerfect package. MOVE the highlighter to the file **GLOBE2_M.WPG** and TYPE **1** or **R** to retrieve the graphic.

```
02-12-91  11:30p              Directory C:\WP51\*.WPG
Document size:        0   Free: 15,255,552 Used:      73,264   Files:      30

     .    CURRENT  <DIR>                  ..    PARENT   <DIR>
     ARROW-22.WPG        187  06-09-90 02:52p   BALLOONS .WPG      3,187  06-09-90 02:52p
     BANNER-3.WPG        719  06-09-90 02:52p   BICYCLE  .WPG        607  06-09-90 02:52p
     BKGRND-1.WPG     11,391  06-09-90 02:52p   BORDER-8 .WPG        215  06-09-90 02:52p
     BULB    .WPG      2,101  06-09-90 02:52p   BURST-1  .WPG        819  06-09-90 02:52p
     BUTTRFLY.WPG      5,349  06-09-90 02:52p   CALENDAR .WPG        371  06-09-90 02:52p
     CERTIF  .WPG        679  06-09-90 02:52p   CHKBOX-1 .WPG        653  06-09-90 02:52p
     CLOCK   .WPG      1,811  06-09-90 02:52p   CNTRCT-2 .WPG      2,753  06-09-90 02:52p
     DEVICE-2.WPG        657  06-09-90 02:52p   DIPLOMA  .WPG      2,413  06-09-90 02:52p
     FLOPPY-2.WPG        475  06-09-90 02:52p   GAVEL    .WPG        887  06-09-90 02:52p
     GLOBE2-M.WPG      7,785  06-09-90 02:52p   HANDS-3  .WPG      1,117  06-09-90 02:52p
     MAGNIF  .WPG      1,023  06-09-90 02:52p   MAILBAG  .WPG      3,353  06-09-90 02:52p
     NEWS    .WPG      1,201  06-09-90 02:52p   PC-1     .WPG      4,035  06-09-90 02:52p
     PRESNT-1.WPG      4,123  06-09-90 02:52p   PRINTR-3 .WPG      1,899  06-09-90 02:52p
     SCALE   .WPG      3,071  06-09-90 02:52p   STAR-5   .WPG        391  06-09-90 02:52p
     TELPHONE.WPG      6,101  06-09-90 02:52p   TROPHY   .WPG      3,891  06-09-90 02:52p
```

The filename is now displayed in the definition and the **Contents** option has changed to **Graphic**.

Instructions

Boxes can be positioned both *vertically* and *horizontally* within the page or paragraph (depending on the type of anchor specified). The options for positioning a box vertically are as follows:

Full Page - The box takes up the whole page or paragraph. Graphics will not be distorted and therefore will not take up the full length of the page/paragraph.

Top / Bottom - The box is positioned at the top or bottom of the page or paragraph.

Centre - The box is positioned in the centre of the page or paragraph.

Set position - The user can determine the exact position between the top and bottom of the page/paragraph.

The *horizontal* position of the box can be set between the margins of a single column document or between the columns of a multi column document. The available options are as follows:

Left - The box is positioned to the left margin of the page or column.

Right - The box is positioned to the right margin of the page or column.

Centre - The box is positioned in the centre between the margins of the page or column.

Full - The box will take up the full horizontal width between the margins of the page or column.

In addition, the user can determine the exact position between the margins of the page or column by selecting the **Set position** option.

Activity 8.4   Positioning and changing the size of a box

The vertical position is already set to **Top** which is the default. To change the horizontal position to **Left** TYPE **6** or **H** to select **Horizontal**, **1** or **M** to select **Margins** and **1** or **L** to select **Left**.

To change the size of the box TYPE **7** or **S**. **Width** and **Height** can be set automatically or set manually. TYPE **3** or **B** to set **Both** manually.

TYPE **1.3** for the **Width** and **1** for the **Height**. The measurements are in inches. *then enter   ENTER*

The definition screen should now resemble the following:

```
Definition: User Box

    1 - Filename            GLOBE2-M.WPG

    2 - Contents            Graphic

    3 - Caption

    4 - Anchor Type         Page

    5 - Vertical Position   Top

    6 - Horizontal Position Margin, Left

    7 - Size                1.3" wide x 1" high

    8 - Wrap Text Around Box Yes

    9 - Edit
```

PRINT   *GRAPHIC APPEAR.*

PRESS `F7` to exit. PRESS `SHIFT + F7` and TYPE **V** to **View** the document. You may have noticed that your picture of the globe is the right way up opposed to the example at the beginning of this task. We will see how to invert a graphic later.

Instructions   Typing text into a box follows exactly the same principles as typing a document on the editing screen. All the same formatting commands can be used. For example, text can be centred, underlined, the font changed, simply by blocking the text and applying the appropriate command.

Activity 8.5   Creating a text box

Make sure the cursor is on the first letter of the 2nd page of COOPER. CREATE a **Text Box** and change the settings to the following:

```
Definition: Text Box

     1 - Filename

     2 - Contents          Text

     3 - Caption

     4 - Anchor Type        Page

     5 - Vertical Position   Top

     6 - Horizontal Position  Margin, Centre

     7 - Size               3" wide x 1" high

     8 - Wrap Text Around Box Yes

     9 - Edit
```

To enter the text into the box TYPE **9** or **E** to enter the **Edit** screen.

CTRL +F8.

TYPE **Down Under Holidays** and use the formatting commands to change the size of the
6 text to 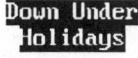 **Very large**, the appearance to **Bold** and the positioning to **Centre**. If you reveal the
codes they should look similar to the following example:

```
           Down Under
             Holidays











Box:  Press Exit when finished, Graphics to rotate text      Ln 0.
{  ▲   ▲   ▲   ▲   ▲]  ▲   ▲   ▲   ▲   ▲   ▲   ▲   ▲
[VRY LARGE][BOLD][Just:Centre]Down Under[SRt]
Holidays[bold][vry large][HRt]
[Just:Full]
```

PRESS **F7** to exit back to the edit screen. It may be a good idea to SAVE your document at this stage.

PREVIEW your document on the screen.

Activity 8.6   Creating a user box

Back in edit mode, your document should look something like this:

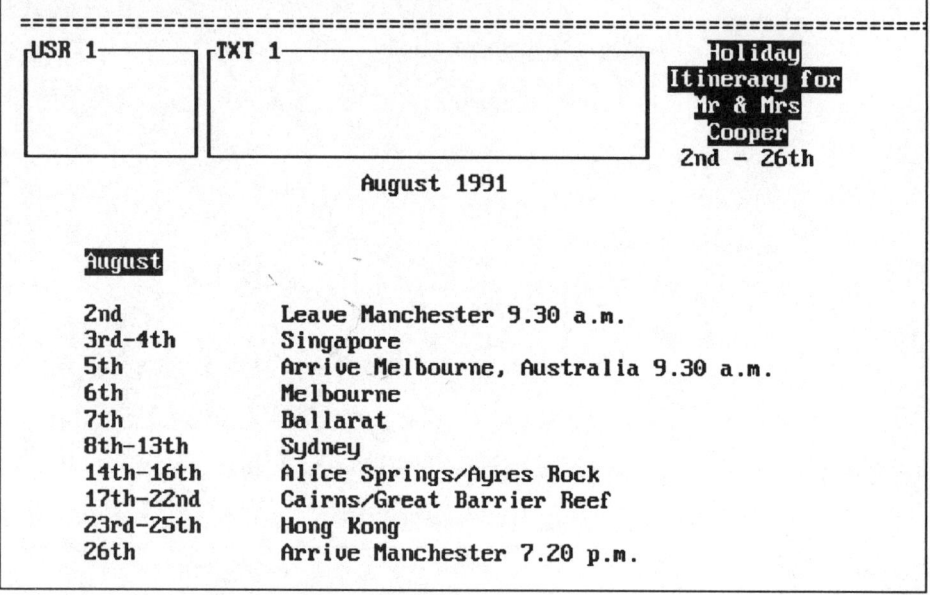

To complete our banner we will create another **User box** positioned to the right of the page. POSITION your cursor on the first character on the page and follow the steps to create a **User box**. CHANGE the settings to resemble the following:

```
Definition: User Box

      1 - Filename              BKGRND-1.WPG

      2 - Contents              Graphic

      3 - Caption

      4 - Anchor Type           Page

      5 - Vertical Position     Top

      6 - Horizontal Position   Margin, Right

      7 - Size                  1.3" wide x 1" high

      8 - Wrap Text Around Box  Yes

      9 - Edit
```

Your edit screen should now show all three boxes:

```
==============================================================================
┌USR 1──────────┐┌TXT 1────────────────────────────────┐┌USR 2───────┐
               ▐Holiday Itinerary for Mr & Mrs Cooper▌
                        2nd - 26th August 1991


               ▐August▌

               2nd          Leave Manchester 9.30 a.m.
               3rd-4th       Singapore
               5th          Arrive Melbourne, Australia 9.30 a.m.
               6th          Melbourne
               7th          Ballarat
               8th-13th     Sydney
```

SAVE and PRINT your document.

Key words
Figure, Text, Table and User Boxes
Definition options
Anchoring

Task 9 Changing the appearance of a graphic

Objective

To *invert* the graphics symbol of the globe.

Instructions

In general, the contents of any box can be changed by pressing `ALT + F9` and selecting the **Edit** option. Select the number of the box you want to change.

Select the **Edit** option from the **Definition** screen. If the box contains a graphic, an image of the graphic will appear on the screen with a menu of options displayed at the bottom of the screen.

Activity 9.1

Changing the size of a graphic

RETRIEVE the document **COOPER** if not already loaded and PRESS `ALT + F9` to access the graphics option.

SELECT **User box** . SELECT **Edit** to change the box definition. You will be prompted for the number of the user box you want to change. TYPE **1** to select the first user box you created, the box containing the globe graphic. The **Current definition** screen will be displayed.

TYPE **9** or **E** to edit the box contents.

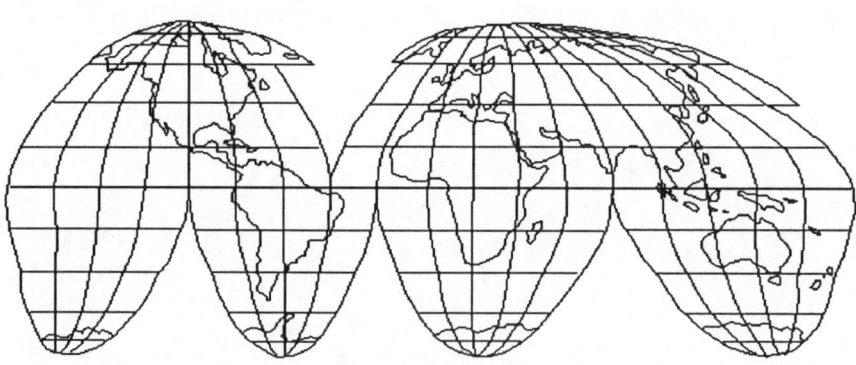

The globe graphic should appear on the graphics editing screen. To change the size of the graphic PRESS `PGUP` to make the graphic larger, and `PGDN` to make the graphic smaller. The size of the graphic will change each time these keys are pressed. To change the graphic back to its original size PRESS `CTRL + HOME`. Experiment with changing the size of the graphic.

Activity 9.2

Changing the position of a graphic

To move the graphic within the box PRESS ← ↑ ↓ →. MOVE the globe to the top of the box and then position it back in the centre.

To rotate the graphic USE the grey **+** and **-** keys on the right of the keyboard.

PRESS the **+** key to rotate the globe clockwise until it is upside down.

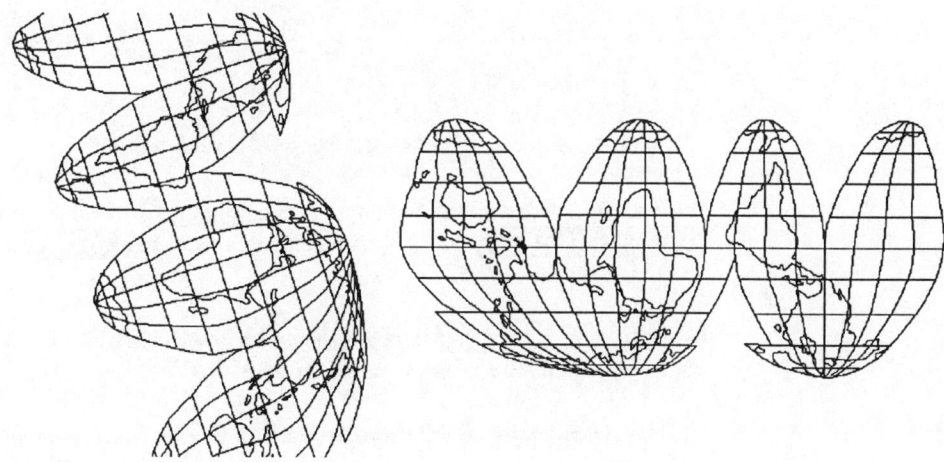

To preserve these changes PRESS **F7** the **Exit** key. PRESS **F7** again to exit back to the edit screen. SAVE your changed document to disk. VIEW or PRINT your document.

Key words   **Move**
              Re-Size
              Rotate

Task 10

Creating and using a template document

Objective

To produce a *template* document that contains the company logo which can be used as a starting point for future documents.

Instructions

Now that we have produced a company logo by using a series of boxes and graphics, it would be useful to be able to call up the logo every time we want to create a new document incorporating the logo heading.

Activity 10.1

Creating a template file

RETRIEVE the document **COOPER2** if it is not already loaded.

The first step is to delete the first page. PRESS `ALT + F4` to block, and PRESS `CTRL + HOME` `↓` to highlight the entire page. PRESS `DELETE` and SELECT the **Yes** option to delete the block.

PRESS `ALT + F3` or `F11` to reveal the codes and DELETE the code for the hard or forced page break. TOGGLE back to normal mode.

MOVE your cursor to the first character *below* the boxes and repeat the above steps to delete all the text on the page.

REVEAL the codes again and DELETE any remaining formatting codes just leaving the boxes with a couple of hard returns below (for blank lines).

```
 ┌USR 1──────┐ ┌TXT 1─────────────────────────┐ ┌USR 2──────┐







                                              Doc 1 Pg 1 Ln 2.67"
{   ▲   ▲   ▲   ▲   ▲   ▲   ▲   ▲   ▲   ▲   ▲   ▲   ] ▲
[Text Box:1;;][Usr Box:1;GLOBE2-M.WPG;][Usr Box:2;BKGRND-1.WPG;][HRt]
[HRt]
[HRt]
```

PRESS `F10` to save the document but *do not* overwrite the original document. DELETE the filename COOPER2 and TYPE **TEMPLATE** instead.

Instructions

Until this point, we have always ensured that we have an *empty screen* before we retrieve a document. This is because WordPerfect will allow a document to be retrieved into another document. If there is a document loaded, the **Retrieve** command will load another document at the cursor position. This is called *merging* documents.

Activity 10.2

Merging an existing document with the template file

RETRIEVE the file **TEMPLATE** if it is not already loaded.

MOVE the cursor to the end of the file and PRESS `SHIFT + F10` to retrieve a document.

Either TYPE the document name, **COOPER** *or* PRESS `F5` for a list of files. PRESS the `ENTER` key to select the directory, HIGHLIGHT the document COOPER and SELECT the **Retrieve** option.

The document COOPER will be *merged* with the template.

SAVE the document overwriting the name TEMPLATE with **COOPER**.

Activity 10.3

Merging the template file with an existing document

An easier method of merging is firstly to retrieve the document and then to retrieve the template.

CLEAR the screen by pressing `F7`. RETRIEVE the document **MEMO**.

Make sure the cursor is at the beginning of the document and PRESS `SHIFT + F10` to retrieve. RETRIEVE the document **TEMPLATE**.

SAVE the file using the same name, **MEMO**.

Instructions

We will now use the template to create a new document that will be used for the next tasks. The document contains •• and spelling mistakes. These are deliberate and will be used to demonstrate WordPerfect's *search*, *replace* and *spell checking* facilities.

Activity 10.4   Creating a new document with the template file

With a clear screen, RETRIEVE the document **TEMPLATE**.

TYPE the text below. The deliberate spelling mistakes are highlighted. Type the text exactly as it appears.

```
Here at ** our one aim is to make sure that you have a holiday
to remember.  Our reprisentatives are on hand 24 hours a day to
answer all your queries and smooth over any problems you may
have.  In fact, we are so confident of our service that our
Managing Director will personally meet with any customer who is
not 100% satisfied and provide a generos package to compensate
for any neglect on our part.

With the benefit of 25 years experience in holiday research and
planning, we are able to offer a comprihensive chose of holidays
to Australia and New Zealand with stop-overs in Asia.  With so
many alternatives to choose from we are sure that you will find
a holiday to suit you. But what if you would like to change part
of a holiday or combine two holidays?  This is where ** earns its
reputation for flexibility.  We can customise any holiday to
accommodate your particular requirements. Our team of Travel
Consultants is available to discuss all your needs and will come
up with a customised itinerary to suit you.

We believe the Consultants at ** to be some of the best in the
industry.  In fact, you don't need to take our word for it. Last
year we were awarded first prize in the National Holiday Service
awards, a highly coverted award in the Travel Industry.

C:\WP51\DATA\DRAFT                                    Doc 1 Pg 1 Ln
```

SAVE the document as **DRAFT**. *Make sure you don't save it as TEMPLATE or you will overwrite your template and won't be able to incorporate it in future documents.*

PRINT your document or VIEW it on the screen to ensure that the logo is situated correctly.

Activity 10.5   This activity is optional and is designed to act as practice for including boxes and graphics within a standard document.

MOVE your cursor to the beginning of the 3rd paragraph, "We believe...".

PRESS **ALT + F9** to call up the **Graphics** menu.

CREATE a **User Box**.

FILL the box with the graphic **CERTIF.WPG**.

ANCHOR the box to the paragraph.

POSITION the box to the right of the paragraph.

Manually CHANGE the width and the height of the box to an appropriate size.

SAVE the settings and VIEW your document to screen. If the graphic is not placed correctly EDIT the box definition and CHANGE the appropriate settings.

SAVE and PRINT your document.

Down Under Holidays

Here at ** our one aim is to make sure that you have a holiday to remember. Our representatives are on hand 24 hours a day to answer all your queries and smooth over any problems you may have. In fact, we are so confident of our service that our Managing Director will personally meet with any customer who is not 100% satisfied and provide a generous package to compensate for any neglect on our part.

With the benefit of 25 years experience in holiday research and planning, we are able to offer a comprehensive chose of holidays to Australia and New Zealand with stop-overs in Asia. With so many alternatives to choose from we are sure that you will find a holiday to suit you. But what if you would like to change part of a holiday or combine two holidays? This is where ** earns its reputation for flexibility. We can customise any holiday to accommodate your particular requirements. Our team of Travel Consultants is available to discuss all your needs and will come up with a customised itinerary to suit you.

We believe the Consultants at ** to be some of the best in the industry. In fact, you don't need to take our word for it. Last year we were awarded first prize in the National Holiday Service awards, a highly coveted award in the Travel Industry.

Key words	Template
	Merge

Section D: Editing and formatting

Task 11   Using the search commands

Objective

To search for *text strings* within a document.

Instructions

When working with long documents it can be very useful to have a feature that allows you to move directly to a chosen place in your document. By selecting the **Search** command you can type a word, sentence, group of characters (referred to as a string) and WordPerfect will move your cursor to that string of characters within the document. For example, you may be proof-reading your document and notice an error. You may have typed *the* twice. Typing *the the* as the search string, will cause WordPerfect to move directly to the first occurrence of that string. There is also a facility to repeat a search if the first occurrence is not the one you are looking for.

In general, position your cursor in the document somewhere *before* the text you are looking for, or at the top of the document if you are not sure where the text is placed.

Press **F2** the **Search** key. Type the text you are searching for and press **F2** again. You need to press **F2** to start the search rather than pressing **ENTER** because you may want to search for a string that contains a press of the **ENTER** key.

To continue a search and look for the next occurrence of the same string simply press **F2** twice.

To change the string you are searching for, press **F2** and edit the search string in the usual way. When finished press **F2** to commence the search.

As well as searching *forward* through your document you can also search *backwards*. If you know that the string you are looking for is close to the end of the document it may be quicker to move your cursor to the end of the document and use a backwards search.

The backwards search works in the same way as the forward search except you Press **SHIFT + F2** to call up the command. Once you have typed the search string, press **F2** to commence searching.

With regard to case, WordPerfect's search feature matches all lower case characters with either upper or lower case; but it only matches upper case characters in the search string with upper case characters in the document. For example, if the search string is **Holiday** you will only find **Holiday** with a capital **H**. If you enter the search string as **holiday** you will find **holiday**, **Holiday** or even **HOLIDAY**.

Activity 11.1   Doing a forward search

With **DRAFT** as the current document MOVE your cursor to the beginning of the text.

PRESS `F2` to search and type **holiday** as the search string.

PRESS `F2` again to commence the search.

The cursor should move to the first occurrence of the word **holiday**. PRESS `F2` twice to find the next occurrence. MOVE through the document finding every occurrence of the word **holiday**.

Activity 11.2   Doing a backward search

MOVE the cursor to the end of the document and PRESS `SHIFT + F2` for a backwards search. SEARCH for all occurrences of the word **Consultants**.

Key words   **Character string / Text string**
Case sensitive
Forward / Backward search
Repeat search

Task 12   Using the replace commands

Objective

To *find* and *replace* a string of characters.

Instructions

We have already seen how to search for a string of characters. The next step is to change those characters once they have been found. This can be an extremely useful feature, especially if you need to change the same information several times. You may have typed a memo about a conference in London which is now to be held in Paris. It is much simpler to change every occurrence of London to Paris than to search through the document manually.

To call up the **Replace** command press `ALT + F2`. Select **Yes** if you want to confirm each change or **No** to let WordPerfect change each occurrence automatically. If necessary, reset the direction of the search and replace. TYPE the string to be replaced and press `F2` to commence replacing.

The **Replace** command can be stopped at any time by pressing `F1`.

You cannot undo a replace so it is a good idea to save your document before replacing. If things go wrong, you can always retrieve your document as it was before you edited it.

Activity 12.1   Searching and replacing

The **Replace** command can be used to save time when typing the same text several times within a document. In the document DRAFT the company name is included several times. To save time, every time the company name should appear, we have typed ●●. We can now replace all occurrences of ●● with **Down Under Holidays**.

SAVE your document.

MOVE to the beginning of DRAFT and PRESS `ALT + F2`. SELECT the **No** option so that WordPerfect will replace automatically. TYPE the replace text as ●●. The search direction is forward which is OK as we are at the beginning of the document.

PRESS `F2` to confirm the search string. You will now be prompted for the replacement text. TYPE **Down Under Holidays** and PRESS `F2` to activate the command. SAVE the document.

Key words   **Replace**
                              Automatic replace

Task 13

Using the spell checker

Objective

To use WordPerfect's inbuilt program for checking the spelling of your document.

Instructions

WordPerfect has an inbuilt dictionary containing 115,000 common English words. When checking the spelling of a document, WordPerfect takes each word in turn and looks it up in the dictionary. If found, it is assumed to be correct. If it is not found, it is assumed to be an error and is highlighted as such. A list of similar words are displayed on the screen and you are given the following options:

Replace - replace the highlighted word with one of the listed corrections.

Skip Once / Skip - choose this option if the word is correct but is not in the WordPerfect dictionary. **Skip once** just skips the current word, **Skip** will skip this and subsequent occurrences of the word.

Add - add the word to your own private user dictionary. In addition to WordPerfect's dictionary you can create your own dictionary to contain names, technical words etc.

Edit - type the word again.

Look Up - look up a word in the dictionary.

Ignore Numbers - tells WordPerfect to ignore all words containing numbers, for example post codes.

The spell checker will also check for improper capitalisation, for example "HEllo" and duplicate words such as "the the". It will not check grammar nor errors in context. For example, it will not flag "there" as an error if it should read "their".

To access the spell checker press **CTRL + F2**. The following options are available:

Word - checks the word following the cursor.

Page - checks the current page.

Document - checks the entire document.

New Supplementary Dictionary - sets up a new user dictionary.

Look up - looks up the word you type.

Count - counts the number of words in your document.

If you SELECT a block before accessing the spell checker, WordPerfect will automatically check the block without offering the choices above.

Activity 13.1   Spell check a document

With DRAFT as the current document, PRESS `CTRL + F2` to access the spell checker.

TYPE **3** or **D** to select the entire document.

Unless you have made any additional typing errors, the first incorrect word should be **Representatives**. The correct spelling is displayed as choice **A**. Type **A** to select this choice.

Continue through the document selecting the correct spellings from the lists.

WordPerfect found all our deliberate mistakes apart from "chose". This is because it is a *context error* rather than a *spelling error*. You will need to use the usual editing techniques to change the word **chose** to **choice**.

Activity 13.2   Spell check a block of text

USE the **Search** command to find the word "Asia". Delete the word "Asia" and type instead, **Hong Kong, Singapore and Thailand.** MOVE further down the paragraph and change the sentence "... earns its reputation for flexibility" by adding the text **and reliabilty** at the end. Misspell reliability!

As we have changed this paragraph we should check the spelling again. Rather than check the whole document we can block the paragraph and just check that.

BLOCK the paragraph in the usual way.

PRESS `CTRL + F2` to call up the spell checker. The block will be checked automatically. The name Hong Kong will be listed as an error. SELECT **Skip** to ignore this error. SELECT the correct spelling for **reliability**.

RE-SAVE the document with the corrections.

Keywords   **Replace**
Skip
Dictionary / User Dictionary
Context

Task 14   Using the thesaurus

Objective

To use the *thesaurus* to find alternative choices for words we have repeated in our document.

Instructions

WordPerfect's thesaurus is a useful feature for widening the vocabulary of your document. WordPerfect will provide a variety of words with the same or similar meaning to the one you select.

To search for alternative words, first position your cursor on the word you want to look up. Access the thesaurus by pressing `ALT + F1`. Choose the most suitable replacement word selecting the **Replace** option and then typing the corresponding letter for the word of your choice.

Activity 14.1

Using the thesaurus

RETRIEVE the document **DRAFT** if it is not already loaded.

MOVE the cursor to the word "suit". PRESS `ALT + F1` to access the thesaurus.

```
holidays?  This is where Down Under Holidays earns it's
reputation for flexibility and reliability.  We can customise any
holiday to suit your particular requirements. Our team of Travel
Consultants are available to discuss all your needs and will come
up with a customised itinerary to suit you.
 suit=(n)
  1 A ·ensemble        5     ·fit
    B ·livery                ·flatter
    C ·outfit
    D ·uniform         6     ·accommodate
                             ·adapt
  2 E ·group                 ·adjust
    F ·series                ·conform

  3 G ·appeal          7     ·accommodate
    H ·entreaty              ·content
    I ·petition              ·please
    J ·plea                  ·satisfy

 suit-(v)              suit-(ant)
  4 K ·agree           8     ·detract
    L ·correspond            ·displease
    M ·match

 1 Replace Word; 2 View Doc; 3 Look Up Word; 4 Clear Column: 0
```

A list of possible alternative words are displayed. In this case there are more choices than can fit into the single column. To choose a word from the second column PRESS the `→` key.

TYPE **1** or **R** to replace and SELECT the appropriate letter to choose **accommodate** (or select your own choice of word).

47

Activity 14.2

Secondary search in the thesaurus

The word "award" has been used three times in the last paragraph of DRAFT. MOVE your cursor to the last occurrence.

PRESS `ALT + F1` to access the thesaurus. The selection of words is not ideal. When this is the case you can request a *secondary search*. For example, let us assume that we believe the word "tribute" to be the best alternative and yet we are not completely satisfied with the choice. We can ask WordPerfect to give us further alternatives for the word "tribute".

TYPE **3** to **Look up word** and SELECT the appropriate letter for the word **tribute**. A second list will appear, something like the following example:

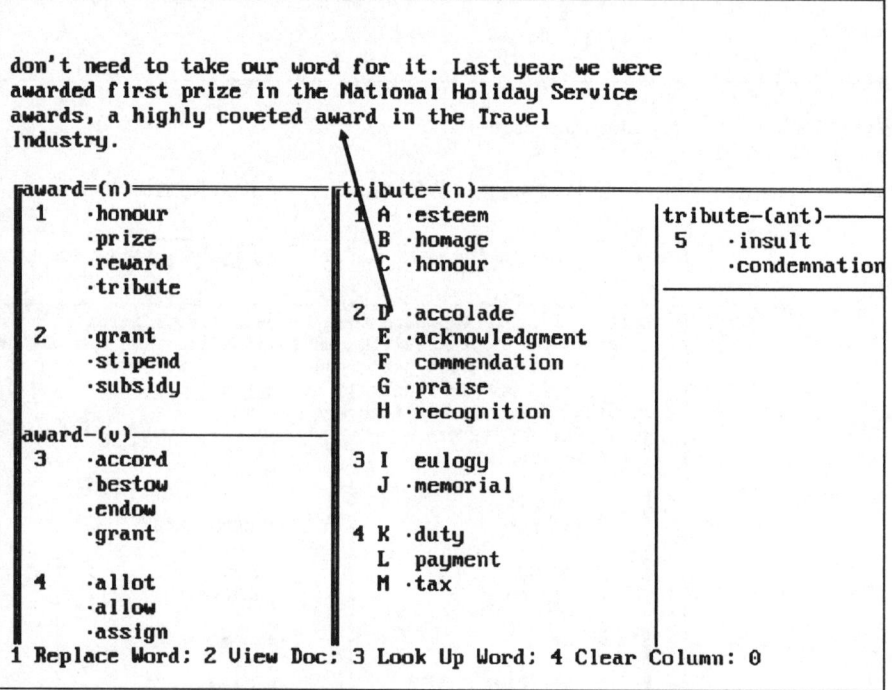

```
don't need to take our word for it. Last year we were
awarded first prize in the National Holiday Service
awards, a highly coveted award in the Travel
Industry.

┌award=(n)════════  ┌tribute=(n)════  ┌tribute-(ant)─────
 1   ·honour         1 A ·esteem       5   ·insult
     ·prize            B ·homage           ·condemnation
     ·reward           C ·honour
     ·tribute
                     2 D ·accolade
 2   ·grant            E ·acknowledgment
     ·stipend          F  commendation
     ·subsidy          G ·praise
┌award-(v)─────        H ·recognition
 3   ·accord
     ·bestow         3 I  eulogy
     ·endow            J ·memorial
     ·grant
                     4 K ·duty
 4   ·allot            L  payment
     ·allow            M ·tax
     ·assign
 1 Replace Word; 2 View Doc; 3 Look Up Word; 4 Clear Column: 0
```

TYPE **1** or **R** to replace and then TYPE **D** to select the word **accolade** or select your own choice from the alternatives.

Task 15

Page formatting: double spacing

Objective

To change the line spacing of our document.

Instructions

The document we produced in the previous tasks is in *draft* form. In order to make space for corrections between the lines we can change the line spacing of the document.

Line spacing can be changed by pressing `SHIFT + F8` and selecting the **Line** option followed by the **Line spacing** command. You will be prompted to type a number. Type 2 for double spacing, 3 for triple spacing etc.

Line spacing can be changed as many times as you like within your document. Each time you change the spacing, a code is embedded into your document in the usual way (see Activity 5.2). The format change will be implemented from that point until the end of the document or until another line spacing formatting code is reached.

Line spacing formatting codes can be deleted by revealing codes and then deleting the appropriate one.

Activity 15.1

Changing the line spacing

RETRIEVE the document **DRAFT** if it is not already loaded.

Make sure that the cursor is at the beginning of the text and PRESS `SHIFT + F8` to access the **Format** options.

TYPE **1** or **L** to select the **Line** options.

TYPE **6** or **S** to select the **Line spacing** option.

TYPE **2** for **Double spacing** and PRESS `ENTER` to confirm.

PRESS `F7` to exit.

USE the **Preview** option to view the document.

The example on the following page shows the document with single spacing and double spacing.

SAVE the document.

Down Under
Holidays

Here at Down Under Holidays our aim is to make sure that you have a holiday to remember. Our representatives are on hand 24 hours a day to answer all your queries and smooth over any problems you may have. In fact, we are so confident of our service that our Customer Director will personally deal with any customer that is not 100% satisfied and provide a generous gesture to compensate for any oversight on our part.

With the benefit of 25 years experience in holiday research and planning, we are able to offer a comprehensive choice of holidays in Australia and New Zealand plus stop overs in Hong Kong, Thailand and Singapore. With so many alternatives to choose from we are sure that you will find a holiday to suit you. But what if you would like to choose part of a holiday or combine two holidays? This is where Down Under Holidays means it's reputation for flexibility and reliability. We can customise any holiday to accommodate your particular requirements. Our team of Travel Consultants are available to discuss all your needs and will come up with a customised itinerary to suit you.

We believe the Consultants at Down Under Holidays to be some of the best in the industry. In fact, you don't need to take our word for it. Last year we were awarded first prize in the National Holiday Service awards, a highly coveted accolade in the Travel Industry.

Single Spacing

Down Under
Holidays

Here at Down Under Holidays our aim is to make sure that you have a holiday to remember. Our representatives are on hand 24 hours a day to answer all your queries and smooth over any problems you may have. In fact, we are so confident of our service that our Customer Director will personally deal with any customer that is not 100% satisfied and provide a generous gesture to compensate for any oversight on our part.

With the benefit of 25 years experience in holiday research and planning, we are able to offer a comprehensive choice of holidays in Australia and New Zealand plus stop overs in Hong Kong, Thailand and Singapore. With so many alternatives to choose from we are sure that you will find a holiday to suit you. But what if you would like to choose part of a holiday or combine two holidays? This is where Down Under Holidays means it's reputation for flexibility and reliability. We can customise any holiday to accommodate your particular requirements. Our team of Travel Consultants are available to discuss all your needs and will come up with a customised itinerary to suit you.

We believe the Consultants at Down Under Holidays to be some of the best in the industry. In fact, you don't need to take our word for it. Last year we were awarded first prize in the National Holiday Service

Double Spacing

| Key words | Single spacing |
| | Double spacing |

Task 16

Page formatting: changing margins

Objective

To change the left and right hand margins of a document.

Instructions

The left and right margins can be changed at any point within a document by pressing `SHIFT + F8` and selecting the **Line, Margins** options. Different margins can be set anywhere within a document. The new margin settings will remain until the end of the document *or* until they are reset.

Activity 16.1

Changing the margins

RETRIEVE the document **DRAFT** if it is not already loaded.

Make sure that your cursor is on the first letter of the text. By placing the cursor *below* the company logo the change of margins will not affect the layout of the graphics.

PRESS `SHIFT + F8` to access the **Format** options.

TYPE **1** or **L** to select **Line** and **7** or **M** to select **Margins**.

TYPE **1.5** for the **Left margin** and **1.5** for the **Right margin**. These measurements are in inches. PRESS the `ENTER` key to confirm each new value.

PRESS **F7** to exit.

Use the **View document** facility to see how the change in margins has affected the document. TYPE **4** to view the document as **Facing pages**, as in the previous example.

Key words   **Left Margin**
                   Right Margin
                   Facing Pages

Task 17   Page formatting: page numbering

Objective   To include *automatic page numbering* in a document.

Instructions WordPerfect can number the pages of a document automatically. As with all other formatting, WordPerfect uses hidden codes to control page numbering. It is important to position your cursor at the top of the first page you want the numbering to appear before entering the code. If the whole document is to be numbered, insert the page numbering code at the beginning of the document.

The page number can be positioned in various positions on the printed page. The steps are as follows:

Move the cursor to the leftmost column at the top of the page where you want the numbering to start and press `SHIFT + F8` to select the **Layout** menu. Select the **Page** option.

```
Format: Page Numbering

    1 - New Page Number        1

    2 - Page Number Style      ^B

    3 - Insert Page Number

    4 - Page Number Position No page numbering
```

Select the **Page numbering** option followed by **Page numbering positioning**. Select an option in the range 1 to 9 to display the page number in the position shown below:

```
Format: Page Numbering

    Every Page                    Alternating Pages

    ┌─────────────┐    ┌─────────────┐  ┌─────────────┐
    │ 1   2   3   │    │ 4           │  │           4 │
    │             │    │             │  │             │
    │             │    │ Even        │  │        Odd  │
    │             │    │             │  │             │
    │ 5   6   7   │    │ 8           │  │           8 │
    └─────────────┘    └─────────────┘  └─────────────┘

    9 - No Page Numbers
```

Activity 17.1   Turning on automatic page numbering

RETRIEVE the document **DRAFT** if not already loaded.

MOVE the cursor to the beginning of the document and PRESS `SHIFT + F8`.

SELECT **Page numbering, Page numbering positioning.** SELECT **6** to centre the page number.

PRESS `F7` to exit. VIEW the document on the screen to see the page number at the bottom of each page.

Instructions   You can change the way the page number is displayed by selecting the **Format** menu, `SHIFT + F8`, followed by the **Page, Page numbering, Page number style** options.

The ^**B** symbol represents the page number. This is entered by pressing `CTRL + B`. To include the page number as Page 1, Page 2 etc you would enter the style as **Page ^B**.

```
Format: Page Numbering

    1 - New Page Number       1

    2 - Page Number Style     Page ^B

    3 - Insert Page Number

    4 - Page Number Position Bottom Centre
```

Activity 17.2   Changing the style of the page number

POSITION the cursor at the beginning of the document. PRESS `SHIFT + F8` and select **Page, Page numbering, Page number style.**

TYPE **Page** , PRESS the `SPACEBAR` once and PRESS `CTRL + B` to enter the page number.

PRESS `ENTER` to confirm and PRESS `F7` to exit. VIEW the document.

Key words   **Automatic page number**
                   Page number style

Task 18   Page formatting: headers & footers

Objective

To include a *header* and *footer* for the DRAFT document incorporating the date and page number.

Instructions

A *header* is text that appears at the top of each page of a document and a *footer* is text that appears at the bottom of each page. Headers and footers can be of any length, but usually one or two lines is sufficient. Page numbers and the date can be included in either the header or footer.

You can create up to 2 headers (called header A and header B) and 2 footers (called footer A and footer B). If both headers or footers are to appear on the same page, one should be left aligned and one flush right to avoid their overlapping. Alternatively, header and footer A could be set to appear on odd pages, and header and footer B on even pages (or vice versa).

The *general* steps for including a header or footer are as follows:

Position the cursor at the top of the page on which you want the header/footer to first appear. This might not be page 1 of your document. You may have title pages that do not require the header/footer information.

Press **SHIFT + F8** to access the **Format** options. Select **Page**. Select either **Header** or **Footer**. Select **A** or **B** for the appropriate header or footer. You will be given 3 options:

Every Page - prints the header/footer information on every page.

Odd Pages - prints the header/footer information only on odd pages.

Even Pages - prints the header/footer information only on even pages.

Type the header or footer information using all the usual formatting commands to position or set the attributes of the text. Leave a blank line above a footer to allow a gap between the text and footer information and a blank line below the header to allow a gap between the header information and the document text.

Page numbering can be included in a header or footer by pressing **CTRL + B** at the point where you want the number to appear. The characters ‸ **B** will appear at the position where the page number will print. If you do decide to include page numbering in the header or footer turn off the automatic page numbering, if on, by selecting option 9, no page numbers, from the **Page numbering position** option (see previous task). If you do not turn automatic page numbering off, the page number will appear twice.

Date and time information can be included by using the **Date/outline** option. Press **SHIFT + F5** and select the appropriate feature (see 3.2).

When finished press **F7** to exit.

Activity 18.1   Adding a header

RETRIEVE the document **DRAFT** if not already loaded.

Make sure your cursor is at the very beginning of the document, the line on which the boxes begin.

PRESS `SHIFT + F8` to access the **Format** options and SELECT the **Page** option.

SELECT **Header** and then SELECT **Header A**.

SELECT **Every page** to print the header on every page of the DRAFT document.

TYPE **Draft Only** and PRESS `ENTER` to leave a blank line.

PRESS `F7` to exit.

SELECT **Header** again. SELECT **Header B, Every page**.

PRESS `SHIFT + F5` to select **Date/outline** and SELECT **Date code**. PRESS `ENTER` to leave a blank line.

Use the **Block** command to highlight the date and PRESS `ALT + F6` to align the date flush right.

PRESS `F7` to exit back to the edit screen. PREVIEW the document.

Header A   *Header B*

Draft Only   1 July 1992

Activity 18.2   Adding a footer

As we are going to include the page number in the footer we need to turn automatic page numbering off. To do this, MOVE the cursor to the top of the document and PRESS `SHIFT + F8`.

SELECT the options **Page, Page numbering, Page number position, No page numbers**. PRESS `F7` to exit.

Make sure the cursor is at the top of the document and PRESS `SHIFT + F8`.

SELECT the options **Page, Footers, Footer A, Every page**.

PRESS the `ENTER` key to leave a blank line above the footer.

To get the page number with a dash either side, (- 1 -), TYPE - (the hyphen key) and PRESS the `SPACEBAR`. PRESS `CTRL + B` to insert the page number. PRESS the `SPACEBAR` and TYPE -.

CENTRE the page number by blocking it and PRESSING `SHIFT + F6` to centre.

EXIT to the edit screen and PREVIEW the document.

```
        reliability.    We   can   customise   any   holiday   to
        accommodate your particular requirements. Our team of



                              - 1 -

```

Footer A

Key words   **Footer**
                  Header

Section E: Printing and macros

Task 19 | **Printing techniques**

Objective | To look at some of the printing options available on WordPerfect.

Instructions | Up until now, to print a document we have pressed `SHIFT + F7` and then selected the **Full** option to print the entire document.

The other options available are listed below:

```
Print

        1 - Full Document
        2 - Page
        3 - Document on Disk
        4 - Control Printer
        5 - Multiple Pages
        6 - View Document
        7 - Initialise Printer


Options

        S - Select Printer              HP LaserJet III PostScript
        B - Binding Offset              0"
        N - Number of Copies            1
        U - Multiple Copies Generated by  WordPerfect
        G - Graphics Quality            Medium
        T - Text Quality                High
```

Activity 19.1 | To print the current page

PRESS `F7` to get a clear screen and RETRIEVE the document **COOPER**.

MOVE the cursor to the second page of the document.

PRESS `SHIFT + F7` to access the print options and SELECT the **Page** option. WordPerfect will print the page on which you have placed the cursor - the *current* page.

Activity 19.2   To print a document from disk

You do not have to retrieve a document to print it. For example, we are currently working with COOPER2 but we may need to print a copy of DRAFT for a colleague.

PRESS **SHIFT + F7** and SELECT **Document on disk** from the options.

TYPE **DRAFT** and PRESS the **ENTER** key.

WordPerfect displays the prompt "Page(s) (All)". PRESS **ENTER** to select all pages. If we had only wanted to print a *selection* of pages we could have typed the page numbers we wanted separated by commas (,).

The document DRAFT will be printed from disk.

To demonstrate the capabilities of your printer, print, from disk, the document PRINTER.TST. This file should have been copied to the sub-directory C:\WP51 when WordPerfect was installed. You will need to type the path, **C:\WP51\PRINTER.TST** as this file is not located in the default directory.

Activity 19.3   To print more than one copy of a document

If you need multiple copies of a document it is quicker to print them in one go rather than individually.

RETRIEVE the file **COOPER** if not already loaded.

PRESS **SHIFT + F7** and SELECT the **Number of copies** option. To save paper we shall TYPE **2**.

SELECT the **Page** option. WordPerfect will print two copies of the page on which your cursor is positioned.

Instructions   When working with longer documents you may want to print a *selection* of pages. To do this, access the print options in the usual way and select the **Multiple pages** option. Type the numbers of the pages you want to print separated by commas e.g: 1,2,6,7 will print pages 1, 2, 6 and 7.

To print a *range* of pages, type the page numbers separated by a hyphen e.g: 12-16 20-25 will print pages 12 through to 16 and pages 20 through to 25.

You can also specify ranges *and* lists of pages, e.g: 1,4,20,25-30.

Entering -20 30- will print pages 1 to 20 and from page 30 to the end of the document.

As all our documents are of limited size there is no Activity to demonstrate this feature.

Key words   **Current page**
                       Multiple copies
                       Printing from disk
                       Selecting pages

Task 20   Macros

Objective

To use the WordPerfect *macro* facility to automate tasks that are carried out on a regular basis.

Instructions

A WordPerfect macro is a program that records a number of keystrokes or menu options so that they can be re-played over and over again. So, by definition, you would only create a macro for a repetitive task.

Macros are best understood by example, but in general terms use the following steps:

PRESS `CTRL + F10` to define a macro. Then give the macro a name. At this stage you need to decide how you want to call up the macro. There are two choices:

Either press `ALT + Letter` where Letter is any character in the range A to Z;

or; type the macro name which can be up to 8 characters in length.

Although it is easier to call up a macro by simply pressing ALT + a letter, this means you are limited to 26 macros, and you have to remember what each macro does.

All macros are saved as *separate* files on disk with the extension M. For example, a macro which is named PRINT would be saved to disk as PRINTM. A macro that is called up by ALT + P would be saved to disk as ALTP.WPM.

It is probably best to define the macros that you use all the time as "ALT" macros, and to name the more specialised macros. In the following activities we shall use both naming methods.

Once you have named the macro you will be prompted to give the macro a *description*. This is *optional*. You can either leave the description blank or type up to 39 characters followed by `ENTER`.

From this point, everything you type and every command you access will be recorded.

Once you have finished, press `CTRL + F10` to stop the macro recording.

To replay the macro *either:* press `ALT + Letter` for macros named with the ALT key; *or;* press `ALT + F10` and type the macro name.

Unless the macro is specific to a particular document it can be replayed when accessing any document. For example, in the next activity we will create macros to save and print a document. These macros can be replayed when working with any existing document.

If you get into a muddle while creating a macro, simply stop the macro by pressing `CTRL + F10` and start again. Type in the same name for the macro and replace the original version on disk.

Activity 20.1   Creating a **Save** macro

One of the most useful macros to have is a save macro. It is advisable to save your documents at least every 20 minutes. Although the necessary steps to save a document are fairly simple it is certainly easier to just press a couple of keys. We shall define this macro as an ALT macro.

RETRIEVE a document.

PRESS `CTRL + F10` to define the macro.

PRESS `ALT + S` to name the macro (the macro will be saved to disk as ALTS.WPM).

TYPE **Save Macro** as the description. PRESS `ENTER`.

From this point, all your key strokes will be recorded.

PRESS `F10` to save.

PRESS `ENTER` to confirm the document name.

TYPE **Y** to replace the old version of the document.

The macro is now complete. PRESS `CTRL + F10` to stop the macro recording.

To run the macro simply PRESS `ALT + S`. Your document is saved to disk!

[This macro can only be used to save documents that have previously been saved to disk and given a name.]

Activity 20.2   Creating a **Print** macro

Another useful macro is one that automatically prints the current document.

Follow the steps outlined in the previous activity and DEFINE a macro named **ALT + P** that will automatically print the entire document. TEST the macro.

Activity 20.3   Creating a macro to enter a signature block

The last two macros have been made up of a series of WordPerfect commands. In this activity we will create a macro that enters text: a standard signature block.

CLEAR the screen using `F7`.

PRESS **CTRL + F10** to define the macro.

PRESS **ALT + N** as the macro name (as we already have a macro called **S** we will call this macro **N** for name).

PRESS **ENTER** to skip the description.

TYPE **Yours sincerely,** and PRESS **ENTER** 5 times.

TYPE your name and PRESS **ENTER**.

TYPE **Managing Director.** UNDERLINE this job title.

PRESS **CTRL + F10** to stop recording and to run the macro. This macro can now be used to sign off all your letters.

Activity 20.4

This final macro example stops part way through a menu sequence to allow the user to type a new document name.

We have already seen how to retrieve the document TEMPLATE and then save it with a new name. This macro will automate the procedure.

CLEAR the screen using **F7**.

PRESS **CTRL+ F10** to define a macro.

This time we will give the macro a name. TYPE **LOGO** and PRESS **ENTER**.

TYPE an appropriate description, for example, **Macro to load the logo**, and PRESS **ENTER**.

PRESS **SHIFT + F10** to retrieve a document. TYPE **TEMPLATE**.

PRESS **F10** to save.

The current document name will be displayed. MOVE the cursor across and DELETE the word **TEMPLATE**.

We will stop the macro at this point to allow the new document name to be entered independently of the macro.

PRESS **CTRL + F10** to stop the macro.

Manually CANCEL the operation by pressing **F1**.

CLEAR the screen and PRESS **ALT + F10** to run the macro.

TYPE the macro name as **LOGO**.

The macro should stop at the point where you need to type in a new name for the document. TYPE **LETTER**. PRESS `ENTER` to confirm the new name.

TYPE the following text after the boxed logo:

Dear Sally,

Thank you for your fax confirming the accommodation for Mr & Mrs Cooper. I have informed them of the change and they are happy with the new arrangements.

Please send me details of price as soon as available.

Finish the letter by calling up the macro for your **signature block**.

Call up the macro to SAVE the document.

Call up the macro to PRINT the document.

Key words	Macro

Task 21   Using temporary macros or variables

Objective

To demonstrate the use of *temporary macros*.

Instructions

The macros we created in the last task are stored *permanently* on disk. You can also create up to 10 macros that are *temporary*. These macros, also called *variables*, are deleted when you exit from WordPerfect.

The temporary macros must be named as ALT + a number in the range 0 to 9, i.e. ALT + 1, ALT + 2.

The macros can only be used to record *text*. They cannot be used to record menu or command sequences. Each macro is limited to 119 characters of text and can be used to hold text strings that are typed several times within a document or series of documents.

In many ways, these temporary macros can be used to the same effect as the replace features looked at earlier. We replaced every occurrence off "***" with "Down Under Holidays". We could have stored the text "Down Under Holidays" as a temporary macro and called up that macro every time the text was needed.

Activity 21.1

Creating a temporary macro

CLEAR the screen.

PRESS `CTRL + PGUP`.

The prompt **Variable:** will appear, TYPE **1** as the variable name (do not PRESS the ALT key).

The prompt **Value:** will appear. TYPE **Down Under Holidays** and PRESS the `ENTER` key.

To call up the macro PRESS `ALT + 1`.

Key words

Temporary macro
Variable
Value

Section F: Mail merge

Task 22

Using the mail merge facility

Objective

To produce a letter to be sent to all our clients using the WordPerfect *Mail Merge* capabilities.

Instructions

The term *mail merge* is usually used to describe the process of merging together a standard letter and a list of names and addresses. In practice, the mail merge capabilities are used for a much wider range of applications, including the production of labels, envelopes, invoices and general lists. For this task, we will concentrate on the mail merge letter and we will start by writing a general letter that can then be used to merge with a list of clients.

Activity 22.1

Creating a new document

With a clear screen TYPE the letter as outlined below. To enter the date, PRESS **SHIFT F5** and TYPE **2** or **C** to SELECT **Date code**. By using date code rather than date text, the current date will always appear on the letter regardless of when it is printed.

```
2 December 1992

Dear Customer

We would like to take this opportunity to wish you a very happy
Christmas and a healthy New Year.

Once the Christmas and New Year festivities are over we are sure
that your thoughts will turn to sunnier climes.  With this in
mind, we have enclosed a full list of brochures that will be
available from January 1st.

To place your order, either call into our office or telephone our
free phone number, 0800 7911.  Your requests will be recorded and
dispatched early in the new year.


Best Wishes


The Team
Down Under Holidays
```

SAVE the letter as **BROCHURE** and CLEAR the screen.

We will now produce what is termed the *secondary file*: the document containing the names and addresses. Each item of information you require for your letter i.e. name, address, town, is referred to as a *field*. Each group of fields is termed a *record*. So, if we have 50 clients to write to, we will need to enter 50 records with each record being made up of a series of fields.

When entering the data for the secondary file, each *field* is completed by pressing
F9 the **End field** key.

Each *record* is completed by pressing **SHIFT + F9**, the **Merge codes** key followed by the **End record** option.

Activity 22.2

Creating a secondary file

To create the secondary file, TYPE the following:

Mrs F9 Cooper F9 10 The Avenue F9 Leeds F9 West Yorkshire
F9 LS6 8YT F9

You do not need to PRESS the **ENTER** key at all.

To complete the record, PRESS **SHIFT + F9** and SELECT the **End record** option. A line will appear across the page.

ENTER another record as shown in the following example.

```
Mrs{END FIELD}
Cooper{END FIELD}
10 The Avenue{END FIELD}
Leeds{END FIELD}
West Yorkshire{END FIELD}
LS6 8YT{END FIELD}
{END RECORD}
========================================================
Mr{END FIELD}
Hughes{END FIELD}
34 New Street{END FIELD}
Bradford{END FIELD}
West Yorkshire{END FIELD}
BD15 4TY{END FIELD}
{END RECORD}
========================================================
```

ADD 2 more records to the list. PRESS **F7** to exit and SAVE the list as **CLIENTS.**

The *next step* is to create the primary merge file by entering the merge fields into the letter. This is achieved by pressing SHIFT + F9 and selecting the **Field** option. You will be prompted to enter the number of the field to be added to your letter. It is important to remember the order in which you entered the fields into the record. The first field in number 1, the second number 2 and so on. In our example title is field 1 and surname is field 2.

Activity 22.3

Creating the *primary* merge file

We have already entered a general letter. We can now use this as a basis for our primary merge file. CLEAR the screen and RETRIEVE the document **BROCHURE.**

To add the client address block, move the cursor to a blank line above the date. PRESS SHIFT + F9 and SELECT the **Field** option. TYPE **1** for the title field.

PRESS the spacebar once to leave a space between the title and surname.

PRESS SHIFT F9 and SELECT the **Field** option. TYPE **2** for the surname field.

ENTER the remaining fields as in the example:

```
{FIELD}1~ {FIELD}2~
{FIELD}3~
{FIELD}4~ {FIELD}6~
{FIELD}5~

2 December 1992

Dear {FIELD}1~ {FIELD}2~

We would like to take this opportunity to wish you a very happy
Christmas and a healthy New Year.

Once the Christmas and New Year festivities are over we are sure
that your thoughts will turn to sunnier climes.  With this in
mind, we have enclosed a full list of brochures that will be
available from January 1st.

To place your order, either call into our office or telephone our
free phone number, 0800 7911.  Your requests will be recorded and
dispatched early in the new year.
```

PRESS F7 to exit and SAVE the file replacing the version on disk.

Instructions

Merging the *primary* and *secondary* files is a simple task. Press `CTRL + F9` for **Merge/Sort** and select the **Merge** option.

When prompted, type the name of the primary file. Press `ENTER`. Type the name of the secondary file and press `ENTER` again.

Once the " * Merging * " message has disappeared from the bottom of the screen, the merged document will be displayed. Each letter appears on a separate page. Use `PGUP` and `PGDN` to move through the letters.

The merged document can be printed in the usual way.

When exiting with `F7` you would usually select the **No** option for saving. It is better to re-generate the merge file rather than save it to disk. There are two reasons for this, first the file will take up valuable disk space, and second, as mail merges are usually a one off operation, you would be unlikely to want to save the file. However, if you do not have a printer attached to your machine you may need to save the merge file so that you can print it on another machine. If this is the case you would select the **Yes** option.

Activity 22.4

Merging primary and secondary files

With a clear screen PRESS `CTRL + F9`.

SELECT the **Merge** option.

TYPE **BROCHURE** as the primary file name. PRESS `ENTER`.

TYPE **CLIENTS** as the secondary file name. PRESS `ENTER`.

When merging is complete, PRINT the letters by pressing `SHIFT + F7` and selecting the **Full document** option.

PRESS `F7` to exit and SELECT the **No** option for saving the document.

Key words

Mail merge
Primary document
Secondary document
Field
Record

Task 23   Adding, changing and deleting records

Objective   To make changes to the secondary file used for the mail merge operation.

Instructions   The data file used for mail merging is the same as a standard document, with the addition of *end of field* and *end of record* codes. Both files are created and edited in the same way.

Activity 23.1   Adding records

With a clear screen RETRIEVE the document **CLIENTS**.

PRESS `HOME` `HOME` `↓` to move the cursor to the bottom of the document.

ADD the following two records to your client list, remembering to PRESS `F9`, the **Field end** key; at the end of each field. PRESS `SHIFT + F9` and SELECT the **End record** option to complete each record.

```
=============================================================
Miss{END FIELD}
Peters{END FIELD}
The Vicarage{END FIELD}
15 Church Walk{END FIELD}
Halifax{END FIELD}
West Yorkshire{END FIELD}
WC12 5UP{END FIELD}
{END RECORD}
=============================================================
Mr{END FIELD}
Josephs{END FIELD}
Primrose Cottage{END FIELD}
Bramhope{END FIELD}
Leeds{END FIELD}
West Yorksire{END FIELD}
LS23 8IT{END FIELD}
{END RECORD}
=============================================================
```

Instructions

These last two records that we have just added, have an additional address field. This is inconsistent with the original records and will cause problems when we merge this file with the letter. In the original records, the town field is Field 4. In the 2 new records, the town field is Field 5. We can make all the records consistent by *adding an extra blank field* to the original records.

If information needs to be changed, for example if a client has changed address, the text can be edited in the usual way.

Activity 23.2

Changing records

With **CLIENTS** as the current document, PRESS `HOME` `HOME` `↑` to move the cursor to the top of the document.

MOVE down to the **Town** field and position the cursor on the first character (L of Leeds).

PRESS `F9` to insert an **End of field** marker above the town field.

Do the same for the next 3 records.

MOVE the cursor to the address line for Mr. Hughes.

PRESS `CTRL + BACKSPACE` 3 times to delete the address. PRESS `←` to move the cursor back to before the end of field marker and TYPE the new address as **34 New Street**.

CHANGE the post code to **BD15 4TY**.

Activity 23.3

Deleting Records

MOVE the cursor to the first character of the third record.

PRESS `ALT + F4` to call up the block feature.

PRESS `↓` until all the fields are highlighted and the cursor is below the end of the record line (on the first character of the next record).

PRESS `DELETE` and TYPE **Y** in response to the prompt, "Delete Block?"

SAVE the document replacing the version on disk.

As we have added a new field to our data file we need to change the primary file, the letter, to include the new field.

Activity 23.4

Changing the primary file

With a clear screen RETRIEVE the document **BROCHURE**.

CHANGE the field definition as below:

```
{FIELD}1~ {FIELD}2~
{FIELD}3~
{FIELD}4~
{FIELD}5~ {FIELD}7~
{FIELD}6~

2 December 1992

Dear {FIELD}1~ {FIELD}2~

We would like to take this opportunity to wish you a very
Christmas and a healthy New Year.
```

SAVE the document replacing the version on disk.

With a clear screen PRESS `CTRL + F9` and SELECT the **Merge** option.

TYPE **BROCHURE** as the primary document name. PRESS `ENTER` to confirm.

TYPE **CLIENTS** as the secondary document and PRESS `ENTER`.

Use `PG UP` and `PAGE DN` to scroll through the merged letters. You will see that the records without a second address field display a blank line. The next task will deal with this problem.

Key words

Adding records
Changing records
Deleting records

Task 24

Eliminating blank lines in a merge file

Objective

To close up the blank lines in the merged letters.

Instructions

When you create a secondary merge file which includes blank field data for one or more records, you must include the **Eliminate if blank** code in the primary document.

Activity 24.1

Including the *eliminate if blank* code

With a clear screen RETRIEVE the document **BROCHURE**.

MOVE the cursor to the ~ character following **{FIELD}4**. Type **?**.

```
{FIELD}1~ {FIELD}2~
{FIELD}3~
{FIELD}4?~
{FIELD}5~ {FIELD}7~
{FIELD}6~

today's date

Dear {FIELD}1~ {FIELD}2~
```

The **?** can be added to any field that is likely to be blank for one or more records. By adding the **?** to the field definition, you instruct WordPerfect to automatically close up the gap if the field is blank.

MERGE the files **BROCHURE** and **CLIENTS**. The blank lines will have been eliminated.

Key words

Eliminate if blank (?)

73

Task 25   Sorting a secondary merge file

Objective

To *sort* our client list into alphabetical order based on surname.

Instructions

WordPerfect has the capability to sort a document in 3 ways:

Line: If a document contains a list, WordPerfect can sort that list *line by line*.

Paragraph: Paragraphs can be sorted into *numeric* or *alphabetical* order.

Secondary Merge File: The records of a secondary merge file can be sorted based on any *field*.

As an example of the sort feature, we will sort the document CLIENTS into alphabetical order based on surname.

Activity 25.1

Sorting a file, part 1

With a clear screen, RETRIEVE the document **CLIENTS**.

PRESS `CTRL + F9`, the **Merge/Sort** key and SELECT the **Sort** option.

The prompt "Input file to sort: (Screen)" will appear. At this point, you can specify a document name or simply PRESS the `ENTER` key to sort the document currently on screen. As we have already retrieved the file that we want to sort, we can just PRESS `ENTER`.

The next step is to specify where the sorted output is to go. There are two choices, *either* the sorted output can appear on your edit screen or it can be saved to a new document on disk. In order to preserve our original data we will save the sorted output to a new file.

In response to the prompt, "Output file for sort: (Screen)", TYPE **SORTED**.

SPECIFY the type of sort by typing **T** to access the **Type** option, followed by **M** to select the **Merge** option. The selected sort type will be indicated on the dotted line half way down the screen.

```
10 The Avenue{END FIELD}
{END FIELD}
Leeds{END FIELD}
West Yorkshire{END FIELD}
LS6 8YT{END FIELD}
{END RECORD}
========================================================================
Hughes{END FIELD}
                                                      Doc 2 Pg 1 Ln 1" Pos
{      ▲      ▲      ▲      ▲      ▲      ▲      ▲      ▲      ▲      ▲      ▲ ] ▲      ▲
----------------------------- Sort Secondary Merge File -----------------------------
Key Typ Field Line Word   Key Typ Field Line Word   Key Typ Field Line
 1   a    1    1    1       2                         3
 4                          5                         6
 7                          8                         9
Select

Action                    Order                     Type
Sort                      Ascending                 Merge sort

1 Perform Action; 2 View; 3 Keys; 4 Select; 5 Action; 6 Order; 7 Type: 0
```

Instructions

Up to 9 sort keys can be specified by selecting the **Keys** option. *Key 1* is the *primary* sort key, *Key 2* the *secondary* sort key and so on. For example, if we had a surname and a firstname field we could select *surname* as the *primary* key with *firstname* as the *secondary* key. If we had a duplicate surname, for instance Smith, by selecting firstname as the secondary key, David Smith would be listed before Peter Smith.

Type - For each sort key we need to specify the type of field we are sorting on. This can either be **a** for alpha or **n** for numeric. Alpha is the default as most fields in a secondary file are alpha fields, fields made up of characters e.g. surname, town. An example of a numeric field might be salary or price.

Field - You also need to specify the number of the field you want to sort on. In our case, if we want to sort on surname, the sort field is number 2, the second field in the record.

Line - As a field may be made up of more than one line of text we need to specify the line number. As all our fields are only one line in length this will be left as 1, the default.

Word - The last option is the word number. If, for example, we had a field called name that contained both first and surname, e.g. James Brown, we might want to sort on the second word, the surname. In our case all our fields are one word in length so we can leave this option as the default of 1.

Activity 25.2	Sorting a file, part 2

In this example, we only need to specify Key 1. TYPE **K** to select the **Keys** option and complete the entry for Key as **a 2 1 1**: The field that we are sorting on is an alpha field (surname), it is the second field in the record, on the first line and is the first word in the field. So, the only thing you should need to change is the field number. As alpha, line 1 and word 1 are the defaults you should not need to change them. MOVE the cursor to under **Field** and TYPE **2** for the second field, surname.

PRESS **F7** to bring the cursor back to the menu line.

If the order is *not* set to *ascending* TYPE **O** for order and SELECT the **Ascending** option. The records will appear in order A - Z. The *descending* option would sort the records in order Z - A.

SELECT the **Perform action** option to initiate the sort.

CLEAR the screen and PRESS **CTRL + F9** and SELECT the **Merge** option. TYPE **BROCHURE** as the primary merge document and **SORTED** as the secondary merge document and PRESS **ENTER**.

The merged letters should appear in order of surname.

Activity 25.3	Practising a sort

CLEAR the screen and RETRIEVE the document **CLIENTS**.

SORT the records by town to a new document called **SORTED2**.

RETRIEVE the sorted file and CHECK that the records are ordered by town.

Key words	Sort
	Primary sort key
	Secondary sort key
	Ascending / Descending order

Task 26

Selecting records for a mail merge

Objective

To produce a *sub-set* of records for clients living in Leeds.

Instructions

If you need to send a letter to a sub-set of clients you can create a new list containing only those records that meet your *criteria*. For instance, if we need to send a letter to our clients in Leeds we can create a new list document by specifying that *Field 5*, the *town* field must contain the word *Leeds*.

It is important to remember that WordPerfect actually *deletes* records that do not match the selection criteria. Therefore, *the output should always be sent to a new file*.

Activity 26.1

Producing a subset of records

With a clear screen RETRIEVE the document **BROCHURE**.

DELETE the body of the letter and TYPE the text below:

```
{FIELD}1~ {FIELD}2~
{FIELD}3~
{FIELD}4?~
{FIELD}5~ {FIELD}7~
{FIELD}6~

today's date

Dear {FIELD}1~ {FIELD}2~

Just a quick note to invite you to our half-yearly travel
seminar. The topics this season include cruises to Australasia,
skiing in New Zealand and self-drive tours of northern Australia.

The seminar will be held on 12th September at the Crossways
Hotel, Leeds. The proceedings will commence at 7.30 p.m. and as
usual cheese and wine will be served throughout the evening.

    Yours sincerely
```

SAVE the letter as **LEEDSLET**.

With a clear screen RETRIEVE the document **CLIENTS**.

ADD **4** new records to the list, **2** for clients in Leeds and **2** for clients in Bradford.

PRESS `CTRL + F9` and SELECT the **Sort** option.

PRESS **ENTER** to select **(Screen)** as the input file.

TYPE **LEEDS** as the name for the output file.

Make sure that **Type** is set to **Secondary merge file** (it should still be set from the previous activity).

SELECT the **Keys** option and set **Sort Key 1** to the **Town** field (if not already set from the last activity). The **Sort key** should read **a 5 1 1** as Town is the 5th field.

PRESS **F7** to exit.

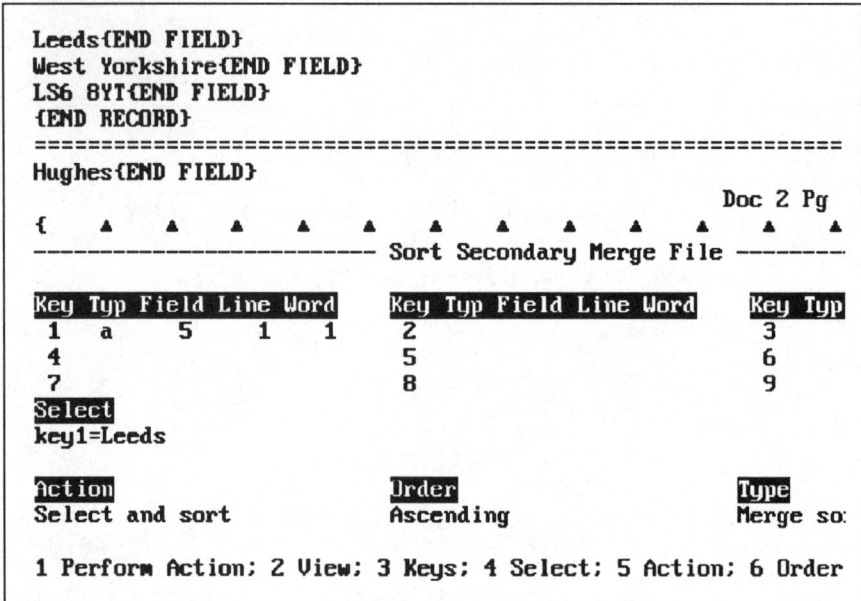

```
Leeds{END FIELD}
West Yorkshire{END FIELD}
LS6 8YT{END FIELD}
{END RECORD}
=============================================================
Hughes{END FIELD}
                                                    Doc 2 Pg
{     ▲    ▲    ▲    ▲    ▲    ▲    ▲    ▲    ▲    ▲    ▲    ▲
------------------------------- Sort Secondary Merge File --------

Key Typ Field Line Word    Key Typ Field Line Word    Key Typ
 1   a    5    1    1        2                          3
 4                           5                          6
 7                           8                          9
Select
key1=Leeds

Action                     Order                      Type
Select and sort            Ascending                  Merge so:

 1 Perform Action; 2 View; 3 Keys; 4 Select; 5 Action; 6 Order
```

CHOOSE the **Select** option.

TYPE **key1 = Leeds**.

PRESS **F7** to exit.

SELECT the **Perform action** option.

CLEAR the screen and PRESS **CTRL + F9** the **Merge/Sort** key.

SELECT the Merge option and TYPE **LEEDSLET** as the primary file and **LEEDS** as the secondary file.

The resulting merge file should only contain letters for clients in Leeds.

Activity 26.2	Practice in producing a subset of records

Activity 26.2   Practice in producing a subset of records

CLEAR the screen and RETRIEVE the document **LEEDSLET**.

EDIT the letter so that the location for the seminar is the **Crown Hotel, Main Street Bradford**, to be held on **25th September**.

SAVE the document as **BRADLET**.

CLEAR the screen and RETRIEVE the document **CLIENTS**.

FOLLOW the instruction in the previous activity to create a new list containing only those clients that live in Bradford.

SAVE this document as **BRAD**.

MERGE the documents **BRADLET** and **BRAD**.

Key words   **Sub-set of records**
Criteria

Section G: Columns and tables

Task 27   Working with columns

Objective

To use *multiple columns* to change the appearance of our DRAFT document.

Instructions

At the moment the DRAFT document is double spaced, with a single column format and margins of 1.5". WordPerfect has the facility to display text in columns. Although 2 or 3 column layouts are most commonly used, you can use a larger number of columns if required. WordPerfect provides two styles of columns:

Newspaper: newspaper columns (or snake columns) start at the top of the first column, continue to the bottom of the page and *snake* up to at the top of the second column and so on.

Parallel: instead of *snaking* from column to column in a continuous flow, parallel columns put related blocks of text next to each other in a tabular format. With earlier versions of WordPerfect parallel columns were used to produce tables. However, version 5.1 has an inbuilt table feature which is much simpler to use (tables are covered in the next task). Parallel columns can still have their uses as we will see in the following activities.

In general, columns can be defined before or after text has been typed. If the text has already been entered, move the cursor to the beginning of the text that is to be put into columns before calling up the columns options with `ALT + F7`.

Select the **Define** option to define your column layout. The following screen will appear:

```
Text Column Definition

    1 - Type                               Newspaper

    2 - Number of Columns                  2

    3 - Distance Between Columns

    4 - Margins

    Column   Left     Right     Column   Left     Right
      1:     1"       3.88"      13:
      2:     4.38"    7.27"      14:
      3:                         15:
      4:                         16:
      5:                         17:
      6:                         18:
      7:                         19:
      8:                         20:
      9:                         21:
     10:                         22:
     11:                         23:
     12:                         24:

Selection: 0
```

The *type* of column can be changed as well as the *number* of columns, the *distance* between the columns and the *margins*. When the columns are defined, press F7 to exit and select the **On** option to turn the columns on.

To turn the column layout off, move the cursor to the end of the column and PRESS ALT + F7 . Select the **Off** option.

As with all WordPerfect formatting, the changes in column layout are embedded within the document as codes. These codes can be deleted in the usual way if you change your mind.

Activity 27.1
2 column - Newspaper style

RETRIEVE the document **DRAFT**. We shall make a copy of this document by saving it with a different name. PRESS F10 to save. SELECT **N** not to replace and DELETE the name DRAFT and TYPE **COLUMNS**. PRESS the ENTER key.

PRESS ALT + F3 or F11 to reveal the codes. DELETE the codes for double spacing and change of margins.

```
            sure that you have a holiday to remember.  Our

            representatives are on hand 24 hours a day to answer

            all your queries and smooth over any problems you may
C:\WP51\DRAFT.WP                                    Doc 1 Pg 1 Ln 2
{       ▲      ▲       ▲       ▲      ▲       ▲       ▲       ▲
[Header A:Every page;Draft Only[HRt]
][Header B:Every page;[Flsh Rgt] ... ][Footer A:Every page;[HRt]
[Centre][-] ^B [-]][Text Box:1;;][Usr Box:1;GLOBE2-M.WPG;][Usr B
G;][HRt]
[HRt]
[HRt]
[Ln Spacing:2][L/R Mar:1.5",1.5"]Here at Down Under Holidays our
ake[SRt]
sure that you have a holiday to remember.  Our[SRt]
representatives are on hand 24 hours a day to answer[SRt]

Press Reveal Codes to restore screen
```

POSITION the cursor at the beginning of the first line of text. This is where we want the columns to start.

PRESS ALT + F7 . SELECT **Columns**. SELECT **Define**.

In this instance we do not want to change the settings so we can just PRESS F7 to exit.

SELECT the **On** option.

Single Column

Double Newspaper Column

PREVIEW the document using **SHIFT + F7**.

Back at the edit screen, REVEAL the codes for the column definition.

```
remember.  Our
representatives are on hand
24 hours a day to answer all                              We belie
your queries and smooth over                             Consulta
C:\WP51\COLUMNS.WP                                       Doc 1 Pg 1
{        ▲      ▲      ▲      ▲      ▲      ▲      ▲
[Header A:Every page;Draft Only[HRt]
][Header B:Every page;[Flsh Rgt] ... ][Footer A:Every page;[
[Centre][-] ^B [-]][Text Box:1;;][Usr Box:1;GLOBE2-M.WPG;][U
G;][HRt]
[HRt]
[HRt]
[Col Def:Newspaper;2;1",3.88";4.38",7.27"][Col On]Here at Do
t]
our one aim is to make sure[SRt]
that you have a holiday to[SRt]

Press Reveal Codes to restore screen
```

Activity 27.2   3 column layout - Newspaper style

DELETE the format codes for the 2 column newspaper layout. The text should return to the single column format.

FOLLOW the procedure outlined in the previous task and set the format to newspaper style **3 column layout**.

3 Column Layout

Activity 27.3   Single and double column layout in one document

In the two examples we have already seen, the entire text is displayed in *multi column format*. This need not be the case. Column formatting can be turned on and off as required.

REMOVE the formatting code for 3 column layout.

POSITION the cursor at the beginning of the second paragraph, CALL UP the column options and accept the default settings. SET the **Columns** option to **On**.

PREVIEW the document. The text in the *first* paragraph is in *single* column format and the remaining text is displayed in 2 columns.

MOVE your cursor to the end of the second paragraph and PRESS **ALT + F7**. SELECT the **Off** option to turn the column settings off. PREVIEW the document. The last paragraph has been moved onto the second page as it would not all fit on the first page.

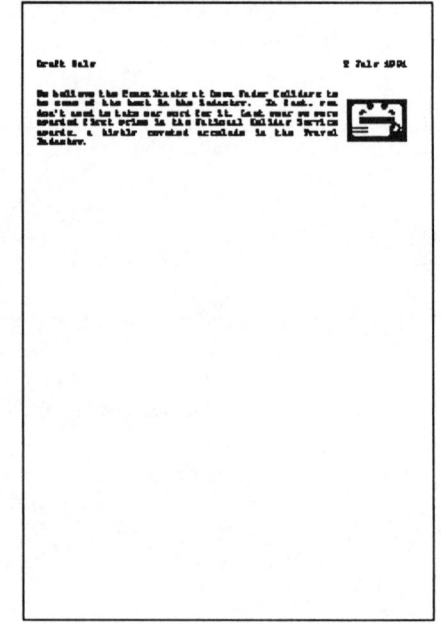

Activity 27.4   Parallel Columns

In the last activity we changed the column layout of the second paragraph. Because the text only filled the one column the second column remained empty. If we want to force some of the text into the second column we will need to use *parallel columns* and embed a forced page break at the point we want the text to move into the next column.

REMOVE the codes for the **2 column newspaper layout**. You will also need to REMOVE the **forced page breaks** that have been entered before the last paragraph.

POSITION your cursor at the beginning of the second paragraph and PRESS `ALT + F7` and SELECT the **Columns, Define** options.

SELECT the **Type** option. There are 2 **Parallel layout** options, **Parallel** and **Parallel with block protect**. The options are similar, the only difference being, the **Parallel with block protect** option will *prevent* a block being split across a page. This means that if a block of text (paragraph) is going to be split across a page, the entire paragraph will be moved to the next page. SELECT **Parallel**. PRESS `F7` to exit and SELECT the **On** option.

At the moment the text looks just the same as with newspaper columns.

Move your cursor to the sentence that begins "This is where Down Under Holidays", half-way through the second paragraph. PRESS `ENTER` to create a new paragraph at this point. PRESS `CTRL + ENTER` to force a page break.

PREVIEW the document. Use your macros to SAVE and PRINT.

| Key words | Newspaper/Snake columns |
| | Parallel columns |

Task 28

Objective

To produce an invoice using the WordPerfect *table* facility.

Instructions

We have already seen how we can produce tables using tabs. The tab method is certainly adequate for some tables. Problems can occur, however, when there is too much text to fit on the one line and the text needs to "wrap" between the tab stops. If this becomes a problem, *tables* are the answer.

A table can be created anywhere within a document by simply placing the cursor where you want the *top left hand corner* of the table to go and pressing `ALT + F7`

You will be prompted to enter the number of rows and columns you want in the table.

At this point the table can be edited, (*rows & columns* added or deleted, *cell widths* changed, *cells* shaded, *line types* changed etc) or you can exit and type the text into the *cells* of the table. The table can be edited at any time by placing the cursor *anywhere* within the table and pressing `ALT + F7`.

[handwritten: BY ENTER]
[handwritten: TABLE 3 Appears you can change to any number Row]

The following activities will cover the steps for producing the invoice illustrated below (the totals will be added later):

Down Under Holidays	
INVOICE	
Mr & Mrs Cooper **10 The Avenue** **Leeds LS6 8TT**	
Flight Manchester – Melbourne return	£1,200.00
Accommodation	£980.00
Excursions	£250.00
Total Exclusive of VAT	
VAT @ 17.5%	
Invoice Total	

Activity 28.1   Creating a table

Starting with a blank screen CALL UP your **LOGO** macro. SAVE the document as **INVOICE**.

ENTER a few blank lines under the logo.

PRESS `ALT + F7` to create a table. SELECT the **Table** option followed by the **Create** option.

TYPE **2** for the number of columns and **10** for the number of rows (extra columns and rows can always be added later).

The table can be edited at this point or after the text has been entered. We will just alter the column widths now and make any further changes after we have entered the text.

With the cursor in the first column PRESS `CTRL + →` until the first column is about three times as wide as the second column (see illustration below).

PRESS `F7` to exit.

Each element of the table is referred to as a *cell*. Each cell can be identified by what is termed a *cell address*. This address is made up of the row and column co-ordinate. *Rows* are labelled by *numbers* 1,2,3 etc and *columns* by *letters* A,B,C etc. The first cell in a table is cell A1. The cell to its right B1 and the cell below A2.

TYPE the text into the cells of the table, pressing the `ENTER` key to start a new line *within* the same cell and the `TAB` key to move *between* cells. FORMAT the cell contents as indicated using the usual editing commands. PREVIEW the document.

Centre, Bold and Very Large

INVOICE	
Mr & Mrs Cooper **10 The Avenue** **Leeds LS6 8YT**	
Flight Manchester – Melbourne return	£1,200.00
Accommodation	£980.00
Excursions	£250.00
Total Exclusive of VAT	
VAT @ 17.5%	
Invoice Total	

Bold (pointing to Mr & Mrs Cooper address)

Flush Right (pointing to the £ amounts)

Bold (pointing to Total Exclusive of VAT)

Bold (pointing to Invoice Total)

Instructions

The ability to join cells is an important feature when formatting tables. To join cells means to remove the boundaries between them. This is useful if you want a heading to display across the top of the table.

Cells can be shaded to enhance the appearance of a table. Shading can also be used to draw attention to a particular cell e.g. a total, sub-total or column heading.

Activity 28.2

Editing the table

With the cursor somewhere within the table, PRESS `ALT + F7`.

JOIN the two top cells by blocking the 2 cells, `ALT + F4`, and selecting the **Join** option from the edit menu. SELECT **Yes** to confirm.

DRAW a double line above the bottom two cells by blocking the 2 cells and selecting the **Lines Top Double** option from the menu.

Use a similar method to draw a double line below the invoice heading and the "Total Exclusive of VAT" line.

MOVE the cursor to the invoice heading line and SELECT **Line Shade** from the menu. SELECT the **On** option. SHADE the 2 cells that will hold the total before and after VAT.

PRESS `F7` to exit and PREVIEW the document. It should look like the one on the previous page.

Key words   **Table**
Cell
Join
Shade

Task 29

Objective

To *calculate the totals* for the invoice created in the previous task.

Instructions

Using the maths facilities

WordPerfect has an inbuilt maths facility enabling you to create formulae based upon values held in a table.

As we have seen, each *element* of a table is referred to as a *cell*. *Formulae* are created by referring to the cell addresses. The current cell address can be found at the bottom of the screen with other cursor information.

We will now insert formulae to complete our invoice.

 **Down Under Holidays**

INVOICE	
Mr & Mrs Cooper 10 The Avenue Leeds LS6 8YT	
Flight Manchester - Melbourne return	£1.200.00
Accommodation	£980.00
Excursions	£250.00
Total Exclusive of VAT	£2.430.00
VAT @ 17.5%	£425.25
Invoice Total	£2.855.25

Activity 29.1   Inserting formulae

Make sure that your cursor is somewhere within the table and PRESS **ALT + F7** to edit.

MOVE your cursor to the cell that will contain the total exclusive of VAT.

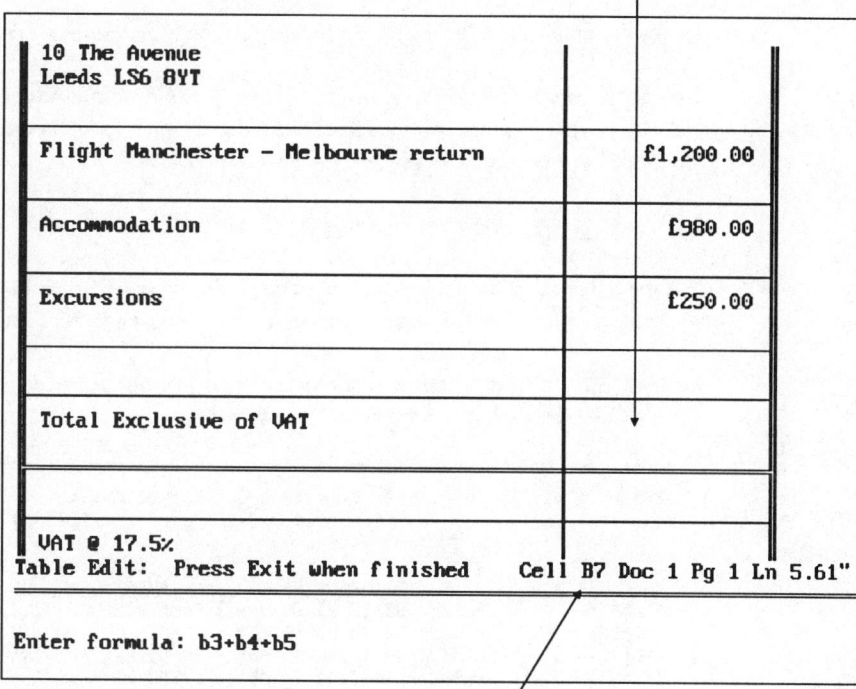

```
  10 The Avenue
  Leeds LS6 8YT


  Flight Manchester - Melbourne return        £1,200.00

  Accommodation                                 £980.00

  Excursions                                    £250.00


  Total Exclusive of VAT                          ↓


  VAT @ 17.5%
Table Edit:  Press Exit when finished     Cell B7 Doc 1 Pg 1 Ln 5.61"

Enter formula: b3+b4+b5
```

This is cell B7 as indicated at the bottom of the screen.

SELECT the **Maths** option followed by the **Formula** option.

TYPE the formula **B3+B4+B5** to add the contents of these 3 cells.

Follow similar steps to ENTER the formula for VAT. VAT is calculated as 17.5% of the Total exclusive of VAT. The formula will be **B7*.175**. ENTER a formula for the invoice total.

EXIT from edit mode and FORMAT the totals for flush right alignment. ADD currency signs by moving the cursor to the appropriate position in the cell and typing the £ symbol.

PREVIEW your document and use your macros to SAVE and PRINT.

Key words   **Maths**
                       Cell Address
                       Formula

Section H: File management and consolidation ▄▄

Task 30

File management

Objective

To use the options available with the *List files* screen to manage our files.

Instructions

The **List files** screen lists the names of the files in a chosen sub-directory or floppy disk. It also includes options to manage those files, including copying, deleting and retrieving. To access the **List files** options press `F5`. You have three choices:

1. Press `ENTER` to view and manage the files in the current directory or disk.

2. Type the name of another disk or directory followed by two presses of the `ENTER` key. This will enable you to view the files but will not make the new directory current.

3. Press `=` and type the name of the new directory or disk followed by two presses of the `ENTER` key. This will make the new directory current.

General Information →

List of files →

Options →

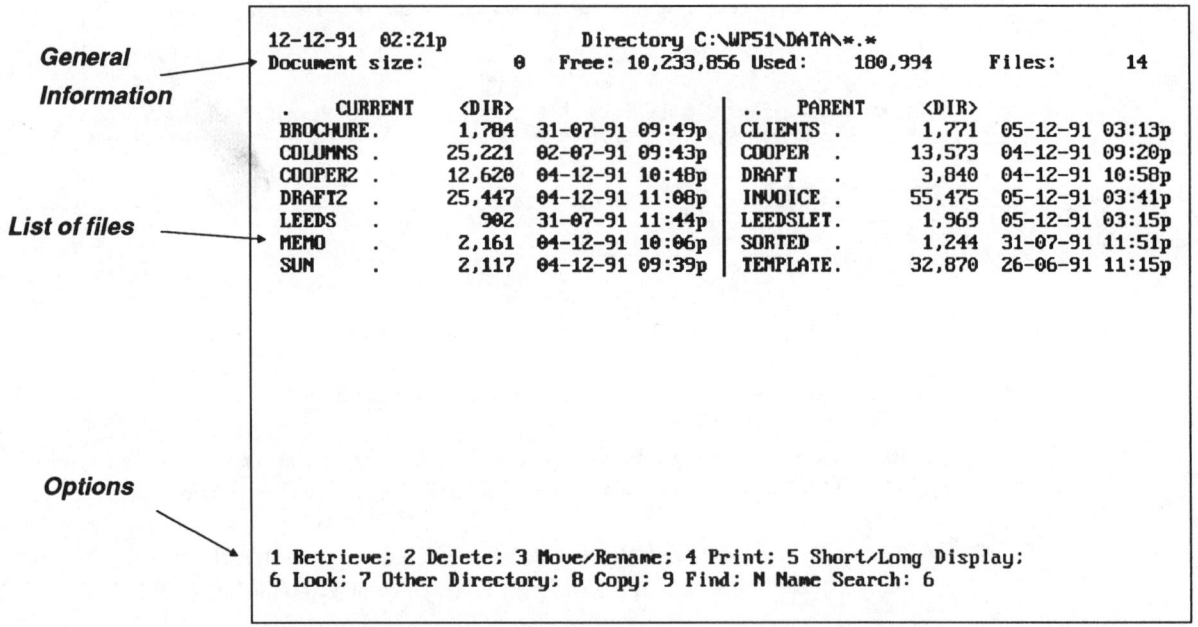

```
12-12-91  02:21p              Directory C:\WP51\DATA\*.*
Document size:          0   Free: 10,233,856 Used:      180,994   Files:      14

     .    CURRENT   <DIR>               ..   PARENT    <DIR>
     BROCHURE.      1,704  31-07-91 09:49p  CLIENTS .      1,771  05-12-91 03:13p
     COLUMNS .     25,221  02-07-91 09:43p  COOPER  .     13,573  04-12-91 09:20p
     COOPER2 .     12,620  04-12-91 10:48p  DRAFT   .      3,840  04-12-91 10:58p
     DRAFT2  .     25,447  04-12-91 11:08p  INVOICE .     55,475  05-12-91 03:41p
     LEEDS   .        902  31-07-91 11:44p  LEEDSLET.      1,969  05-12-91 03:15p
     MEMO    .      2,161  04-12-91 10:06p  SORTED  .      1,244  31-07-91 11:51p
     SUN     .      2,117  04-12-91 09:39p  TEMPLATE.     32,870  26-06-91 11:15p




 1 Retrieve; 2 Delete; 3 Move/Rename; 4 Print; 5 Short/Long Display;
 6 Look; 7 Other Directory; 8 Copy; 9 Find; N Name Search: 6
```

The **List files** screen is divided into three parts:

General information - displayed at the top of the screen, the general information includes the current date and time, the name of the directory, the current document size, the amount of space used by the files and the number of files in the directory.

List of files - the files are listed in alphabetical order, displaying the file name and extension (if one has been given), the size of the file and the date and time that the file was last saved to disk.

Options - the available file managing options are listed at the bottom of the screen. To access any of these options, move the cursor to highlight the required file and select the option. The default option is option 6, **Look**. If you highlight a document name and press `ENTER`, the contents of the document will be displayed.

The available options are listed below:

Retrieve - We used this option in task 2 to retrieve a document. If you know the name of the document you want to retrieve it is often easier to press `SHIFT + F10` and type the document name. If you are unsure of the name, use this option to retrieve your documents.

Delete - If your directory becomes cluttered with documents that you no longer need, use this option to delete them.

Move/Rename - This option allows you to move a document to another directory or disk or give an existing document a new name. When selected, the current document name and directory are displayed. To rename the document, overtype the document name. To move the document, overtype the directory or drive name.

Print - We have already used this option in task 19 to print a document from disk.

Short/Long Display - By default, the directory is displayed in two columns. This is the **Short** display. The **Long** display shows the directory as one column.

Look - The Look option allows you to view the contents of a document without retrieving it. This option is the default.

Other Directory - This option was used in the Getting Started section of this text to create a new sub-directory to save our documents.

Copy - This is a useful option if you want to make a copy of an existing document.

Find - If you remember some details of the content of a document but you cannot remember the document name, you can search through the documents for a specific word or phrase. To find out more about this option use the help feature. Select the option and press `F3`.

Activity 30.1 Managing files

The **List files** options can be displayed whether you have a file loaded or not. PRESS `F5` to view the current directory. PRESS `ENTER` to confirm that you want to use the current directory.

If you have saved documents on the hard disk of your machine, MOVE the cursor to highlight **BROCHURE**. SELECT **Move/Rename**.

PUT a diskette into drive A of your computer. TYPE **A:\BROCHURE** and PRESS `ENTER` to confirm. The document will be moved to the diskette in drive A. BROCHURE will no longer be listed in the current directory, it has been moved to the floppy diskette.

HIGHLIGHT **INVOICE.**

SELECT **Move/Rename.** MOVE across and change the document name to INVCOOP. PRESS `ENTER` to confirm.

The document will be renamed to INVCOOP.

HIGHLIGHT **INVCOOP** and SELECT **Copy**. You will be prompted for a new name. TYPE **INVTEMP**. You should now see two documents in the list, INVCOOP and INVTEMP.

We will now delete the document INVTEMP.

HIGHLIGHT **INVTEMP** and SELECT **Delete**. A Yes/No prompt is displayed. SELECT **Yes**. Delete any other files that you no longer require.

Key words	**Delete**
	Rename
	Move
	Copy

Task 31

Consolidation exercise

Objective   To consolidate the knowledge gained in the last 30 tasks.

Instructions   This last activity pulls together a number of the WordPerfect features introduced in this guide. If necessary, refer back to the relevant tasks as you work through.

Activity 31.1   CREATE a new document called **GENERAL**

Either include the *Down Under Holidays* company logo at the top of the document or CREATE your own company logo.

TYPE the following text:

General Information

Choosing the Right Holiday

Our brochures are full of exciting holiday destinations with stop-overs in a number of locations. Choosing the right combination can be a daunting task. Make sure that you utilise the services of our experienced staff to the full. In each of our offices there will be at least one Travel Consultant who has visited the hotel of your choice. Make an appointment to meet with them and come armed with questions.

There are also a series of videos available showing all the destinations and hotels included in our brochures. These can be borrowed, free of charge. Simply ask at your local office.

Cancellation

We are unable to refund deposits if a holiday is cancelled by the client. Furthermore, if a holiday is cancelled within 30 days of the holiday date, cancellation charges may be incurred. For full details on cancellation charges, please refer to your booking form.

Travel Insurance

We advise all clients to purchase adequate holiday insurance. Down Under Holidays can provide a policy to suit any holiday duration and destination at a special reduced price for clients booking their holiday over 4 months in advance. Ask your Travel Consultant for details.

If you decide to organise your own insurance, be sure to study the small print!

Passport and Visa Requirements

All passengers must be in possession of a 10 year British passport, valid for at least 6 months beyond your planned return date.

Currently, British tourists need an entry visa to visit Australia and it is the responsibility of all clients to ensure that they have obtained this visa from the Australian Consulate.

Health Regulations

Although no vaccinations are currently required for entry into Australia, clients planning a stop-over in Asia may well need a number of vaccinations. It is the responsibility of the client to ensure that the health regulations of the country to be visited are complied with.

Baggage

A baggage allowance of 23kg is allowed for all passengers travelling tourist class. Excess baggage will be charged at the current rate.

We recommend that each passenger carry no more than one suitcase and one item of hand luggage. Hand luggage must comply with the airline standards. Details will be made available with the issue of tickets.

Check-In Times

Passengers are reminded that check-in time is 2 hours before departure for all international flights. Due to security procedures, passengers will be unable to check in baggage any later than 45 minutes before the flight.

Activity 31.2

Edit the document

SPELL CHECK your document (remember to SAVE it first).

CENTRE the document title. INCREASE the size of the title and use the formatting attributes to make it **bold** or **shadowed**.

UNDERLINE the paragraph headings.

INCLUDE the date and the title "General Information" as a header.

INCLUDE the page number as a footer.

PREVIEW and SAVE the document.

INCLUDE the graphic **SCALE.WPG** within the section on baggage. EMBED the graphic **CLOCK.WPG** within the last paragraph, "Check-in times". Include the graphic **MAGNIF.WPG** somewhere within the "Travel Insurance" paragraph.

PREVIEW, SAVE and PRINT the document.

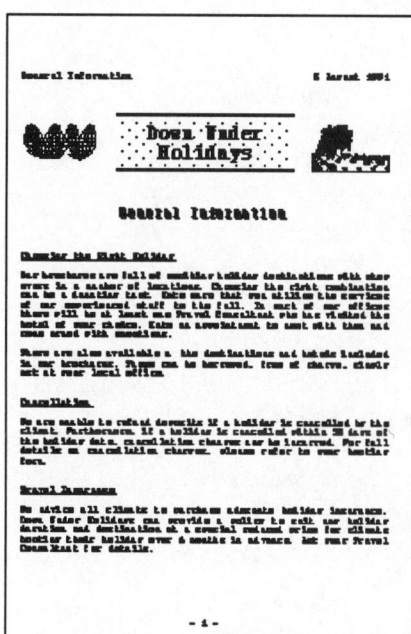
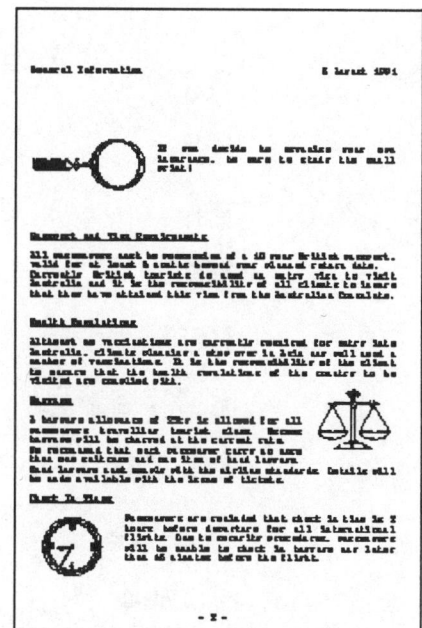

CHANGE the document to 2 column layout. PREVIEW, SAVE and PRINT.

Appendix 1 - Keyboard Shortcuts

Moving Around a Document:

→	Right a letter
←	Left a letter
↑	Up a line
↓	Down a line
HOME ←	Beginning of line
HOME →	End of line
CTRL + →	Right a word
CTRL + ←	Left a word
PAGE DN	Next Page
PAGE UP	Previous page
CTRL + HOME ↓	Bottom of page
CTRL + HOME ↑	Top of page
HOME HOME ↓	Bottom of document
HOME HOME ↑	Top of document
HOME ↓	Bottom of screen (can also use grey + key)
HOME ↑	Top of screen (can also use grey - key)
CTRL + HOME Page No	Specific page
CTRL + HOME Char	Specific character

Deleting text:

BACKSPACE	Character to left of cursor
DELETE	Character at cursor position
CTRL + BACKSPACE	Word at cursor position
HOME BACKSPACE	From cursor to the beginning of word
HOME DEL	From cursor to the end of word
CTRL + END	From cursor to the end of line
CTRL + PAGE DN	From cursor to the end of page
F1 R	Cancel last deletion

Appendix 2 - Function Keys

		CTRL	SHIFT	ALT
F1	Cancel	Shell	Setup	Thesaurus
F2	Search →	Spell	← Search	Replace
F3	Help	Screen	Switch	Reveal Codes
F4	Left Indent	Move	Centre Indent	Block
F5	List	Text in/out	Date/Outline	Mark Text
F6	Bold	Tab Align	Centre	Flush Right
F7	Exit	Footnote	Print	Columns/Tables
F8	Underline	Font	Format	Style
F9	End Field	Merge/Sort	Merge Codes	Graphics
F10	Save	Macro Define	Retrieve	Macro

F11	Reveal Codes
F12	Block

Whatever package...

there is a
TRAINING GUIDE
to suit your needs

Each title follows the same effective format:

- text is fully comprehensive yet jargon free

- the authors approach is reliable, clear and consistent

- covers all the main functions of the package

- useful, quick Index and Glossary

Ask for the titles in the Pitman Publishing TRAINING GUIDE series in your local bookstore. Alternatively, contact our marketing department:

Pitman Publishing
128 Long Acre
London WC2E 9AN
Tel: 071 379 7383

DATABASES
Ami Pro 2
dBASE III
dBASE IV
DataEase 4
Fox Pro 2
Paradox 3

DESKTOP PUBLISHING
Aldus PageMaker 3.0
Aldus PageMaker 4.0 for Windows
Quark Xpress for Windows
Timeworks 2
Ventura Publisher 2.0
Ventura Publisher 4.0 for Windows

SPREADSHEETS
Lotus 1-2-3
Lotus 1-2-3 2.3 & 2.4
Microsoft Excel 4.0
Multiplan
Quatro Pro 3
Smartware
SuperCalc 4 & 5
SuperCalc 5.5

WORD PROCESSING
Locoscript 1.5
Microsoft Word for Windows 1.1
Microsoft Word for Windows 2.0
WordPerfect 5.0
WordPerfect 5.1
WordPerfect 5.1 for Windows

INTEGRATED PACKAGES
Microsoft Works 2
Symphony 2

ACCOUNTING PACKAGES
Pegasus
Sage Bookkeeper
Sage Financial Controller

OPERATING SYSTEMS
Ms-Dos 1-4
Ms-Dos 5.0
Windows 3.0 & 3.1
UNIX

FROM START TO FINISH

This major new series offers its readers complete and thorough mastery of the most widely used databases, spreadsheets, desktop publishing and word processing packages.
Suitable for use by absolute beginners, each title will take the student through every aspect until they have achieved a significant level of competence. The format and structure of the books enable students to follow one learning strategy (and use only one book) for preparation for the series of examinations they need to pass.

- covers all functions and applications of each package
- geared to the needs of the student who wishes to pass examinations after each learning stage
- a one-book solution to learning a package from elementary to advanced levels
- accompanying 3.5" and 5.25" disks are available for each title

Titles include:

dBASE IV 1.1
Lotus 1-2-3 for Windows
Word 2.0 for Windows
PageMaker 5 for Windows
Quark Xpress 3.1 for Windows
WordPerfect 5.1 for Windows

Ask for the titles in the **From Start to Finish** series in your local bookstore.
Alternatively, contact our local marketing department:

Pitman Publishing
128 Long Acre
London WC2 9AN
Telephone: 071 731 2622

OPEN LEARNING SERIES

This user-friendly series provides clear, step-by-step instructions to all aspects of each package. Many college courses are now based upon **open learning** techniques and an increasing number of people are developing word processing skills at home or in the office.

- purpose written open learning material
- task centred, with helpful guidance notes
- clear, easy-to-follow instructions
- each unit is self contained to allow 'dip-in' learning for those requiring spot revision
- a problem-solving section in each unit answers questions for those learning alone

Titles include:

WordPerfect 5.1 for DOS and Windows
Microsoft Word for Windows 2.0
Lotus 1-2-3 for Windows
dBASE IV 1.5

Ask for the titles in the *Open Learning Series* in your local bookstore. Alternatively, contact our Marketing Department:

Pitman Publishing
128 Long Acre
London WC2E 9AN
Tel: (071) 379 7383

Announcing an end to complex manuals
and expensive training courses

Introducing

HOW TO TRANSFER
YOUR SKILLS IN...

WORD PROCESSING SOFTWARE
Microsoft Word for Windows 2.0; Microsoft Word 5.5
WordPerfect 5.1; WordPerfect for Windows 5.1;

SPREADSHEET SOFTWARE
Lotus 1-2-3 2.4; SuperCalc 5; Excel 4; Quatro Pro 4

DESKTOP PUBLISHING SOFTWARE
Ventura 4.0 for Windows; Ventura GEM 3.0;
PageMaker 4; Timeworks 2.0

DATABASE SOFTWARE
dBASE IV 1.5; Fox Pro 2; Paradox 3.5; DataEase 4

All titles by Lea Weston

This best selling series is an essential reference for anyone wishing to use more than one software package. Succinct and easy to handle, these titles work with what you already know and provide the direction needed to transfer to another package.

" ... Lea's book is original and constructive and one I would recommend to all temporary word processing operators and secretaries"
- *Amanda Jackson, La Creme Secretarial Recruitment Consultants*

"An innovative, user-orientated book ... I recommend it"
- *Jack Whelan, The Mackit Partnership*

Ask for the titles in the **How To Transfer Your Skills** series at your local bookstore. Alternatively, contact our marketing department:
Pitman Publishing, 128 Long Acre, London WC2 9AN.
Telephone: (071) 379 7383